INVITE

The Great Dr James Dane

to your next

Function, Conference

or Seminar.

He is an accomplished speaker, with a gifted

sense of humour, and loves to share his knowledge about male/female relationships.

Contact Details

Phone: +61 413000180

Email: greatdane@westnet.com.au

TO ORDER COPY OF THIS BOOK

Go to website:

www.doctorjamesdane.com

or Email: greatdane@westnet.com.au

You can also follow him on Facebook under

James Dane

CONTENTS

Chapter 1
WHAT IS A BLOCKHEAD   1

Introduction   1

Further description of blockheads   2

Why do men act like blockheads?   3

Let's get serious for a bit   4

Book is mainly about differences between males and females   5

It contains general guidelines only   6

For whom is this book written   7

Book is about the basics   7

Chapter 2
THE BUCK STOPS WITH YOU, BIG DOG   9

You need to take responsibility   9

ABOUT THE BOOK

Hello ladies. What on earth are you doing here? Didn't you see the warning sign on the door? Don't you know I wrote this book for beginners and blockheads, who I'm just trying to domesticate so you don't have to put them in the Doghouse? It's a lonely place you know.

Okay, so you want to change your man (maybe even for a different one – God forbid). Yes, I'm sure you have told him about your needs many times over, but he won't listen – right! In fact, one could say that he has even been given a book about everything he needs to know – YOU. All you're really trying to say is that you love him, and need him to love you back.

Well, why not give another man a go – ME. No, I don't mean trade him in. Rather, just give him this book. It has plenty of humour, and was written by a man who understands things about your man. After all, it takes a blockhead to understand another blockhead doesn't it?

It's all about mystery stuff – that is, as far as men are concerned. Who knows, you may even discover a few hidden mysteries yourself. So what about buying this book for him or leaving it somewhere he can see it? He is at least going to like the title.

Men, if you actually bought this book for yourself you probably don't need it as much as some. However, if your partner gave it to you, it's going to unlock a few things about women that may just blow your mind. My mind was blown away, by what I discovered about the opposite sex, when I was about twenty six years old.

About the book

The book is about what I have learnt about women over a forty year period through personal experience, observation, research, and contemplation – and by endeavouring to put certain principles into practice.

Men, be warned, the book contains dog themes. Please don't be offended, but I had to get the message across using the closest analogy I could find to describe men's behaviour. I would now like to share the knowledge I've gained with you. It can be a dog of a life without it.

Good luck, and I hope the book helps someone, somewhere, somehow.

Regards

James

Chapter 3

PUPPY LOVE 13

You need to make a woman FEEL loved 13

Not done by using logic or lecturing 15

So what is the answer? 15

Acts of kindness 17

Thoughtfulness 18

Affection 21

A woman needs to feel special 22

Sweet talk makes a woman feel loved 23

Give them their own money 25

Some things to avoid 26

Chapter 4

PRETTY POODLE AND PIT BULL DIFFERENCES 28

How women differ from men 28

Scientific studies comparing male/female brains 30

My observations 32

Exaggerated gender differences 32

Chapter 5
DON'T TREAT A CAT LIKE A DOG 40

Don't treat a woman like a bloke (man) 40

Don't rush her 42

A man should let a woman release her feelings 43

    1) Offer solutions 45
    2) Invalidate her feelings 46
    3) Tell her to pull herself together 47
    4) Go brain dead 47
    5) Walk away 48

Women are easily hurt 49

Be careful with your use of words 50

Don't be blunt or too open 54

Chapter 6
ROTTWEILER GUIDE TO LOVE AND SEX 56

Three mysteries about sex explained 56

The first mystery 56

For a woman love and sex are not separate 58

Don't be too direct 59

Where does sex begin for a woman? 59

Other reasons women say they don't want sex 60

Twenty ways to guarantee a sex free marriage 61

More detail a man needs to know	62
1) Affection without sex	62.
2) Don't be too needy	62
The second mystery of sex	63
The third mystery of sex	64

Chapter 7

WOMEN SOMETIMES FEEL CRAZY, BUT DON'T TAKE IT PERSONALLY   66

Premenstrual tension	66
Don't take it personally	68
Learn to recognise the signs	70
Take some pressure off her	71
Control your emotions	71
Don't inflame the situation	73
Don't attack or insult the person	74
Never, never insult your partner...	75
What to do if a woman goes silent	76
Understand that women feel better when they vent their feelings	77

It's the time she needs your love the most 78

Chapter 8

SO YOU LOOK LIKE A GREAT DANE 79

The kind of man a woman likes 79

A woman likes a man who is responsible 80

A woman likes a man who is understanding 80

A woman likes a man who is clean 81

A woman likes a man who smells nice 82

A woman likes a man who is loving 82

A woman likes a man who is confident 83

A woman likes a man who has money and is generous 84

A woman likes a man who stands up for himself with other men 86

A woman likes a father, who helps with the kids 87

A woman likes a man who is real 87

A woman likes a man who is in touch with his female side 88

A woman likes a man who is not too heavy 89

A woman likes a man who is strong emotionally 90

A woman likes a man who is good with his hands 91

More about the kind of man a woman likes 91

Chapter 9

ARE YOU A DOG OR A MOUSE? 93

A woman does not respect a man who caters to her every whim 93

Be careful 94

It's all about love and sex 95

Chapter 10

DON'T BE FREAKY 97

Don't be a control freak 97

The insecure controller 98

The little Hitler 102

The controller who sees everything as a power struggle 105

    1) Low self esteem 105
    2) Feelings of disrespect 106
    3) Pride 107

Chapter 11

DON'T BE MR PLASTIC 108

Don't try too hard to be what you are not 108

Women like men who are real 109

Chapter 12

MORE STUFF TO KEEP YOU OUT OF THE DOGHOUSE — 112

Other helpful tips for men — 112

Women need to feel connected — 113

Sometimes a woman would like you to read her mind — 115

Don't treat a woman like an object — 116

Need to spend time with your partner — 117

Women need to feel needed — 119

Women don't want to be your mother — 120

Late is a four letter word — 121

A woman will learn your ways — 121

Women need someone who is always there — 123

    1) Your physical presence — 123
    2) Your love — 123
    3) Your support and encouragement — 124
    4) Your emotional stability — 124
    5) Your commitment — 125

Chapter 13

THE 20 COMMANDMENTS FOR PIT BULLS   126

For men only   126

Chapter 14

BORING STUFF   130

It's about plain hard work   130.

It kills romance   131

It makes her moody   131

Women can lose respect   132

So what can we do to ease the pressure?   132

WHAT IS A BLOCKHEAD

Chapter 1

Introduction

Before I get too far into introducing the topic of this book, I think I better start off by explaining a little about one of the terms on the front cover – the term blockhead.

Men, let's face it, we are all a little dumb when it comes to male/female relationships, and, to be frank, at times we act like plain blockheads – which for the purpose of this book I define as a man who is devoid of such things as love, feeling, sensitivity, knowledge and understanding, regarding the opposite sex. A blockhead is also defined a man who is given good advice about how to treat his partner, yet the information goes in one ear and straight out the other. Some might say, "it's more like he's got a hollow head rather than a blockhead made of wood." Well, maybe.

Further description of blockheads

1) A man who clumsily stomps on a woman's toes on the dance floor, and when she screeches he throws his hands in the air in bewilderment and says, "What's wrong with you now?"

2) A man who wonders why his wife got upset just because he said she was fat and looked like a big bag of potatoes.

3) A man whose smoker breath smells like a chimney, gets around the house with a face full of shabby unshaven whiskers, smells of BO – and yet has no idea why women don't like him.

4) A man who gets intoxicated at a party, and thinks it's a great old joke to spontaneously push his wife (who had just been showing off her new evening dress and hair style) into the swimming pool. He then wonders why she didn't get the joke.

5) A man who eagerly jumps into bed with his wife for his usual two minute sex. A bit like a Rottweiler.

6) A man who's total preoccupation is beer, football, sex and using the F-word.

7) A man who treats his partner like he is a little Hitler.

8) A man whose understanding of women is dumber than dumb.

9) A man who has no concept about the state of his relationship with his partner, and is bewildered when it falls apart.

10) In general, men who do or say things to women that are received by them as well as a pork chop in a synagogue.

11) A married man who spends most of his life in the doghouse.

Now, I think at this stage of this book, I can hear women who are reading it, with the intention of giving it to their husbands, beginning to get excited – but just hold off a bit because I haven't really got to the straight talk yet in the chapter entitled "The 20 Commandments for Pit Bulls", towards the end of the book. I just hope, when you read that section, you don't think the book would have been better called, "Blockhead to Blockhead Guide for Better Marriage".

Most men, of course, don't do the type of things I've mentioned above (do they?). However, they do similar things in accordance with a blockhead type mentality, which will be discussed in later chapters.

Why do men act like blockheads?

Well, because they are men and not women I guess. Basically it boils down to a lack of knowledge. By that I mean, knowledge concerning the physical, mental and psychological differences between a man and woman – which is the main subject matter of this book.

I remember, when I was in my twenties, reading my first book on male/ female relationships. What I learnt at the time blew my mind, and made me realise how many mistakes I had been making with the opposite sex. Since then, 34 years of passive meditation about the subject have passed by – and it was after that time I decided to study the subject intently in preparation for this book. As a result, I realised even more the many differences between men and women. Some things I discovered were to me no less than profound, and will be covered in the proceeding chapters.

To use a modern analogy, understanding women and treating them in the proper way is a bit like operating a computer. You need to know what you are doing. Press the wrong buttons, and not only will your woman go crazy, but you may end up losing your marbles as well.

Let's get serious for a bit.

Today one of the greatest tragedies facing humans on this planet is the pain and suffering of marriage breakup. It has driven many people to the point of murder, suicide and mental breakdown. Words simply cannot describe the heartbreak, emptiness and sadness that it causes, not only for the husband and the wife involved, but also for the little fragile hearts of children. It simply should not be, but unfortunately it is another hard reality that many humans experience on planet earth. The sad thing about it is that in some cases it may have been avoided if the man involved had realised that he needed to take the lead and educate himself. That is, educate himself about some of the differences between men and women, as well as learn some principles, regarding how better to treat them. Instead, regarding this subject, many men are still in bubs and remain close minded. They may have advanced academically, gone through university and become skilled in their jobs, become experts in football and cricket, but unfortunately have never been exposed to some profound basic knowledge that every man should know – how to treat a woman. It's this knowledge that should be taught to young men before ever entertaining one of the biggest responsibilities they could ever take on – that of getting married and having children. Deep within the hearts of men is a dream of living happily ever after with a quiet, consoling, compassionate, soft, caring and sweet lady. Well, it's really a bit of a fairy tale, but if they would like to be on the receiving end of anything like that kind of love from a woman they need to at least educate themselves about the subject covered in this book – otherwise, their life could finish up miserable and shipwrecked.

The book is mainly about differences between males and females

This book is by no means a cure-all for bad marriages, but mainly covers just one aspect. It's about understanding some of the basic differences between you and your lady partner, and advises how to treat her in a better way. It is understood that often there is not much hope of saving many bad marriages because of many other issues. For example, some marriages breakdown simply because of incompatibility or the traits and personalities of the couple's involved. In other cases, the marriage has deteriorated to the point of no return. However, believe me, understanding the differences between men and women is basic, and adjusting your behaviour accordingly can sometimes make a big difference in a marriage or relationship. So, if this book has a part in saving or improving just one marriage, my mission will be accomplished, and it will give me sheer delight.

It contains general guidelines only

This book contains GENERAL GUIDELINES only, which may not always apply in every marriage or relationship, but will apply to a lot of situations, and therefore are handy to keep in mind. At the very least, it will give you a few things to look for, and hopefully help you to better understand your partner/wife and treat her in a better way. Of course, every woman is a unique individual, and should be understood and treated accordingly, and not according to general gender difference. However, the knowledge of gender differences in this book can help you to identify why things may not running as smoothly as they could.

It is also not the purpose of this book to necessarily PROVE that every last principle and piece of advice contained therein, if implemented, will actually work. A lot of what I have written is my opinion based on my life experience as well as what I've researched. Obviously, I'm convinced of what I have written. What I suggest is that you try some of the principles you think may apply to your situation, and see if it works.

My main purpose is simply to pass on what I have learnt and experienced over a forty year period. However, I will provide as much supporting evidence as I can to back up various points I make – but hopefully, it will be self evident that most points have merit and are worth thinking about.

For whom is this book written

Well, for beginners and blockheads of course, as suggested by the title. And yes, it has got a dog theme to it, so if you find yourself displaying a few Rottweiler or Pit ball characteristics you may be able to learn a few new tricks. Yes, even if you are an old dog. However, unfortunately it will probably be only women and good hearted men who will read this book, while men who have really thick blockhead mentalities will not be interested. Holding onto blockhead mentalities is not bliss, but more like banging your head against a brick wall over and over again. It's sad, and hurts both the man and the woman involved in the relationship.

The book is also written for young men (beginners), who are not experienced in relationships, so that when problems arise they will have some idea of what is going on and some clue about how it can be handled.

The book is about the basics

Many books have been written about relationships between men and women based on real life experience, but the first place to start is with some basic principles. These basics are simple, but powerful and life changing if applied. However, they need to be studied – not just read. They need to be studied like any other academic subjects that you have studied at school or university.

You also need to keep thinking about them over a lifetime until it becomes like riding a bike.

It is not my intention in this book to go much further than these basics, although I have added a bit of detail to wet your appetite and give you an idea of how much there is to know about this subject – and why you need to know. It is therefore strongly suggested that you further educate yourself by reading other books with more detail and case histories.

Men, remember I am a man too, and that we are all in the same boat. It can be a dog of a life without this knowledge, and time in the doghouse can be lonely. So let's get started. Good luck!

THE BUCK STOPS WITH YOU, BIG DOG

Chapter 2

You need to take responsibility

So you want to be the big dog. At least you want your partner/wife to make you feel like the big dog – right! Well, I guess men dream about those things. However, if you want to feel anywhere near that level of respect from your partner, you need to take responsibility for the success of the relationship. Accordingly, the first principle to be understood, if a man is having problems in his relationship and wants to make it better, is that it starts with HIM taking the responsibility. He should not leave it to his wife. It's my experience that women don't really like to feel like big dogs. No, I strongly suggest the man not put all the responsibility for the success of the relationship on the shoulders of his wife or partner. A man needs to start taking the lead, mainly by setting a good example – and subjecting his partner to the type of love that fulfils a woman's needs (their needs are different to yours, and puppy love will be explained later). He needs to get the ball rolling. A good place to start is by examining HIMSELF, and seeing what HE can do to improve the situation.

Unfortunately, all too often men are too preoccupied with blaming their wives for the problems in their relationship, while at the same time being totally oblivious to what they are doing or not doing to hinder the happiness and success of their relationship. For example, in a lot of bad marriages, men are often just turned off by their wives reactions, and don't stop to consider if they are contributing to the situation or whether they can do anything to break what may be a bad downward spiral.

Instead of trying to understand their wives, some men, who are managing their marriages very badly, become numb to their wives feelings, and easily slip into the blockhead mentality I described earlier. In other words, they become desensitised to their partner's feelings. Sometimes, their understanding seems to go no further than thinking that their wives are mental cases, and by doing so absolve themselves of any responsibility for the not so nice reactions they receive. The tendency is to blame their wife for everything to do with the bad relationship, while being blind to their own shortcomings – no matter how blatantly obvious those shortcomings are to everyone else around them.

Unfortunately, this head in the sand approach is a recipe for disaster. Now, please don't get me wrong. By saying all this, I'm not saying that women are always justified in their reactions, but what I am saying is that unless men take on the responsibility for improving the relationship, to be blunt, chances of things improving, in my opinion, are pretty much ZILCH. Men, you can either dismiss what I'm saying as just a bigoted or over dogmatic opinion or you can try what I'm about to suggest, and see if you still think the same. The suggestion is that you start taking responsibility for improving the relationship by educating yourself in man/female relationships, and then see if there is anything you can do to improve the situation. Please just forget about your wife for a while, and start by improving the SELF – the MAN in the house (hopefully, you are not a mouse. At least try not to squeak).

One way a man can start educating himself is by reading a few books about the subject. If your relationship is particularly bad, this simple act will probably have immediate results. The first thing that may happen, when you start bringing books about male and female relationships into the house, is that you may find your wife's eyes light up with astonishment. She might even start cheering – that's if she doesn't just faint. Men, don't knock it. I especially recommend bringing this book you are now reading into your house. Another book that I thoroughly recommend is entitled "What Women Want Men to Know" by Barbara De Angelis. It was written by a woman, and consists of feedback from about a thousand women. Even though, after reading it, you may feel you are married to them all at least you may learn a few things. The book that I read when I was about

26 years of age was entitled "Letters to Philip" by Charlie W Shedd. I recommend it, and you can probably track it down on the web. Another good book is "Men are from Mars Woman are from Venus" by John Gray. Only, in my opinion, some parts get a bit over complicated. If you have trouble finding any of these books, I suggest you search such websites as: www.amazon.com on the internet. Who knows, by bringing a few books into your house you may even get lucky that night. However, you can't stop there because it is only the beginning. You see, if you want more sex, than what may happen as a result of bringing a few books in the house – you need to take responsibility throughout your whole life, never stop learning, and "gradually" apply some of the things you learn. So please don't close this book yet because we have only just started, and so far it wasn't as hard as you thought it was going to be, was it now?

PUPPY LOVE

Chapter 3

You need to make a woman FEEL loved

Men, you may be the big dog in the family, but unless you give your partner a little bit of puppy love you will be neglecting one of a woman's basic needs. And no, I don't mean panting like a puppy and giving her a sex starved look when you come home. Rather, you need to know how to make a woman feel loved.

One of the most hurtful experiences for a woman is to be in a relationship with a man who does not make her FEEL loved. I cannot emphasise the word FEEL enough. A woman sometimes only knows that you love her when she can feel it. Deep down you may love her, and have provided for her physical needs, such as a nice house. You may have put food on the table, bought her things like a fridge, washing machine and other items for the house. You may have even bought her a car, got her a job, paid for her education and sacrificed your time by working long hours to ensure your family's future welfare and security. And yes, those things are needed, and may be expressions of your love. They are also things that may need to be done before it becomes possible for a woman to 'feel loved'. However, making a woman feel loved is often achieved by communicating a softer type of love, which she also needs. Some men with high doses of male hormones might say, "oh you mean that lovey dovey mushy stuff". Others might call it puppy love. Well, yes I guess, and I will explain more about what that entails later in this chapter. But the plain truth is that providing her physical needs and leaving the other stuff undone will usually not make her feel loved, and she will sense something is missing.

I read a book recently by a woman, who interviewed over a thousand women, and then wrote about what they wished men knew about them. In the book I was amazed at how many times the female author mentioned how women 'feel' this and that. She particularly mentioned how women are "feeling people". I have also noticed this to be true myself over the years. Yes, men have feelings too, but it seems that women generally are more sensitive. They are particularly sensitive to what their male partner says or omits to say/ does or omits to do – whether it is perceived in a positive way or negative way.

If a man knows what words and actions make a woman feel loved she can blossom like a rose and be as sweet as sugar.

However, if she doesn't feel loved she'll shrivel up, and may even turn very bitter. She will also cry a lot on the inside and outside.

Unfortunately, a man can be a little dumb about how to make his partner feel loved, and some men don't care. If this is the case with you, it is extremely important that you now open up your mind.

Not done by using logic or lecturing

Some men have tried using logic to convince their wives that they love them. However, what they don't seem to understand is that a woman often can't be made to feel loved simply by a man using logic and reason. In fact, when a man tries this, instead of feeling loved, a woman may feel lectured or that the man is talking down to her. Consequently, instead of convincing her of his love, all that often results is an argument or both people getting hurt feelings.

Sorry, but merely telling a woman that you love her, and not understanding or doing the things that make her feel loved will not work. No matter how good your intentions may be.

So what is the answer?

What then makes a woman feel loved? Well, the good news is that the answer is not only simple, but easy to do. You see, it's not so much the big or expensive things you give her that make her feel loved, or the hard decisions that you have to make for the long term welfare of the family etc. Rather, it's more to do with the small things you say and do every day, that cost little or nothing at all.

MEN, please sit up and take notice. Did what I said really sink in? What I'm telling you is PROFOUND, not to your wife, but to a man, if he really has the eyes to see. If you have not really thought about this before, you have absolutely no idea about the power you possess to improve your relationship by simply doing little things for your partner on a consistent basis. If there is just one thing you gain from this book, let it be this one. It's the TINY LITTLE THINGS that a man does that makes a woman feel loved. Right now, I would like to grab you and shake you, so you really understand how POWERFUL doing these small things can be. Not only can doing these things sometimes hide a multitude of mistakes and blunders a man makes with a woman – but can change a relationship almost overnight. In other words, it can change the way a woman FEELS – sometimes instantaneously. So what are the types of little things that can have such a dramatic effect and make a woman feel loved?

A man makes a woman feel loved by doing things such as: small acts of kindness, giving affection, being thoughtful, being considerate and doing acts that communicate that she is special. Another name for it is T L C – tender loving care. Most women thrive on it. Doing all those sorts of things on a day to day basis earns brownie points, and sends a strong message that you love her. She can feel it. A man also needs to follow up, from time to time, by telling his partner that he loves her – as well as saying other sweet endearing complimentary words, spoken with sincerity and a good heart (sweet talk). But beware! Unless those words are preceded by those little acts of love on a consistent basis, they may fall on deaf ears, and there is no way she will believe you. Sorry men, but unless you come up with the real deal, so she can feel it, your words will be wasted. They need to be combined with actions.

Having introduced this subject, I now need to fill in a few details so that you get more of an idea of what I mean. Every woman of course is different, and you need to see what works with your own partner and what does not. In this chapter I have listed some common examples of things that they like, dare I say, in most cases. I have put them under various headings.

The encouraging thing is that a lot of these things are not that hard to do, and will probably have immediate good results. However, let me warn you. You may find it hard to understand why women like some of those little things so much and why they have such a good effect. The reason for this is simple. Men and women are different (in case you hadn't noticed). Not only do they look different, but they are wired differently and have different NEEDS. So men, don't try too hard to understand it. Just accept it, and use it for mutual advantage. You just need to get to know your partner, and see what small things make her eyes light up, make her feel good, touches her, softens her and makes her feel loved. When a man sees a woman's positive reactions to the little things he does for her, it should gradually become something more natural for him to do. In fact, it should become a pleasure like any other form of giving (but only do it to your wife/partner. You can still be a man with a man – okay!).

See now the following list, which is organised under various headings:

Acts of kindness

1) Making her a cup of tea or coffee at home, or asking her if she would like a drink when you go to a party.

2) Opening the door for her occasionally.

3) Carrying something heavy for her.

4) Doing practical things like: washing the dishes, vacuuming the house or bathing the kids, when she is under pressure

5) Giving her a break from cooking by taking the family out to eat occasionally.

6) Making her breakfast

These small acts are all part of making a woman feel loved and cared about. Unfortunately some men give up on some of these things as time goes by for one reason or the other. Yes, I don't know the circumstances in the relationship in which you find yourself. However, generally speaking, if the relationship has any chance at all, I suggest you don't stop, but take a deep breath, and continue to encourage your partner's sweet side. Doing these little things is not rocket science, but shows that you care about her. I know it's not always easy because of the enormous pressures of life, but somehow you need to dig deep, and do these things willingly, and from a good heart.

Thoughtfulness

A woman often feels loved because of a man's thoughtfulness. When I say thoughtfulness, I mean the kind of thoughtfulness that caters for a woman's needs (not a man's). Following, is a list of the type of thoughtful acts that makes a woman feel loved:

1) Remembering things like birthdays and anniversaries.

2) Giving the type of gifts ladies like (not men like) on their birthdays and anniversaries etc. You know, personal gifts – something cute, pretty or romantic. Things like flowers, jewellery, a dress, a purse etc. No men, probably not a washing machine, fridge, iron or cake mixer. I know you may do it out of a deeper kind of love because of the practicality of such items, but unfortunately it would probably not be appreciated on those occasions. Save that kind of love for another time. And yes, buying some of those practical things usually costs a man more money and maybe he has a heart of gold, but unfortunately, it might just go down like a lead balloon. In her eyes, you bought something for the house, and not for her. Buying her a small piece of jewellery, instead of a big washing machine for her birthday, will make her feel special. She will feel loved. If you don't understand why – don't try. She is a woman, not a man. You can't fight it and you can't change it. You just need to accept it, and treat her accordingly.

3) Buy her something for no reason, like a bunch of flowers or some things you know she likes. One book I read once described doing that kind of thing as expressing fragments of your devotion. In other words, they are expressions of your love for her, and it will add up to her feeling loved. Doing those things can also sometimes help cover a multitude of your sins, so to speak. And, sometimes a BIG bunch of flowers can really soften a woman's heart and help reconcile a relationship that has suffered a setback.

4) When you plan something or ask her to go out somewhere, you need to give her the time she needs to do all the little things ladies need to do to prepare – particularly if you are asking her to go on a trip or to a formal night out. I remember many years ago, when I was a young single man and attended a particular church, the single men were encouraged to take out the single ladies. One such opportunity was asking them to go to a church dance. Unfortunately, being so young, I was not experienced with women and so sometimes, in typical male blockhead-like fashion, I would put off asking them out to such occasions until the last moment – after having had weeks or months to do so in advance. You know, a bit like asking one of your mates if he wants to go down the pub for a drink. I don't know whether I actually asked anyone to a formal church ball at the eleventh hour, but I would not have put it past some of us young men to do so at the time. Well, to my bewilderment, the response to this type of request was likely to be an angry NO – probably even if lady concerned had nothing else to do.

This often left us young men feeling rejected, deflated and it affected our self esteem. You see, we thought we were doing something nice by inviting them, but what we did, in our ignorance, was to make the ladies concerned feel that we did not care one whit about them. Apparently, I was not too bad looking back then, but, after receiving this type of reaction, you could have fooled me. At one stage I remember feeling quite depressed and thinking that ladies were not attracted to me. Little did I realise it was not because of looks women reacted that way, but because of my thoughtlessness. Some ladies might say: "it's a bit like a man has a block of wood inside of his head instead of a brain".

Men, asking a lady to go to a ball or an overseas trip at the last moment, after having had weeks and weeks to do so, is like suddenly fronting up with a pork chop in a synagogue and thinking you are doing the people a favour. The reaction is not good. Just don't try it. The moral of the story is that men need to think about where they are asking a woman to go, and give her enough time to do all the little things she needs to do in order to be prepared. The fact is that women need much more time to prepare than men. They are usually more detail minded, and need time to do things like: picking out a dress to wear, getting their hair and nails done etc. Apart from that, when you just drop it on them at the last moment, after having weeks to tell them, they do not feel particularly flattered. A woman may also feel rather low on your list of priorities, and as a result feel unloved.

Now, as I mentioned at the beginning of this book, I was very fortunate to have begun reading about male/female relationships when I was 26 years of age, and so I gradually learnt from my mistakes. It is therefore a sad thing for me to observe some older men, who unfortunately were never exposed to this subject when they were young, making the same mistakes I made in my early twenties. Year after year they continue their thoughtless blundering approach towards their partner. To those men I exhort: start understanding women's needs, and realise they are different to men's needs. Consider the type of occasion you are asking them to attend, and treat them with the thought and consideration women appreciate.

Affection

With regard to little acts of affection, once again, I am not talking rocket science, but you would be amazed at how many men have badly neglected or given away this aspect of their relationship. No, marriage is not just one great long hot Hollywood romance year after year, but if you want to encourage your partner to be sweet you need to make her feel loved by giving her affection. So what do I mean? Yes, it's different in every relationship, but here is a bit of a guide:

1) Give her a kiss when you go to work and when you come home. Sometimes make the kiss longer than six seconds. Somehow it has a good effect on women. They feel loved.
Give her a little kiss or hug throughout the day – especially when you sense she needs one or would appreciate it.

2) Hold her hand sometimes when you go out. Put your arm around her at parties when you are sitting together.
3) Acts of affection don't have to be big. They can simply be a caring hand or a pat on her shoulder.
4) Put your arm around her when in bed.

Men, work it out yourselves, but understand that women need affection – some more than others. No, marriage is not one long sizzling romance and changes as you get older, but affection, to one degree or another, needs to remain part of the relationship if you want to make your wife feel loved.

A woman needs to feel special.

Another very important principle that men need to keep in mind, regarding how to make their partner feel loved, is to understand that a woman needs to feel special in your life. One woman, on the internet expressed it this way: *"Simply put, women need to feel loved. A women feels loved when she is number one in her partner's life. She needs to know he values her over the job, friends, co-workers, hunting, golf, his mom, and the kids. If a woman perceives she takes second place in any area of her man's priorities, she will start to build a wall that protects her emotionally. She will pull away and not see her man as a safe person she can trust with all of her vulnerabilities. If she does not feel safe and loved by her man she will then begin to deny her need to feel loved, or worse, get the need met by someone else. Either way the relationship suffers when this dynamic occurs and will often lead to the relationship ending. Again I will say, in order for a woman to feel loved she needs to feel first in her man's world."*

A man needs to keep the above in mind, and consider very seriously whether he is spending too much time away from his wife doing other things. It's all part of making a woman feel loved.

Sweet talk makes a woman feel loved

Men, how would you like a sweet little lady in the house? Okay, so we know that nobody is perfect, but why not work at doing the things that help bring out her sweet side. Sweet equals sweet and if you know how to talk sweet to a woman chances are she will respond and be sweet back. If you make her feel sweet enough times, she will grow to believe it, and her sweet side will want to show itself. But talk nasty, feed her negative thoughts, put her down, criticize her, and guess what you will receive back. What you say about her will probably become true, and be a self fulfilling prophecy.

When I had a job as a security guard for a short while, one of the techniques we were encouraged to employ in order to pacify disorderly women was sweet talk. Yes, sweet talk, using terms such as, love, darling, sweetie etc. They are words that many of those women had probably have never heard anyone say to them before. It worked, and the reason it did was because women thrive on sweet words, and it makes them feel good about themselves.

It also helps calm their mood and soften their attitude. Women love feeling that you approve of them, and so sweet talk also involves complimenting them on their hair, their dress, shoes and general appearance. It also includes complimenting them on their cooking and showing appreciation for other things they do for you. It's all sweet talk to them, and sends a message that you approve of them and love them.

The other incentive for learning about these little acts of love is that they often cover a multitude of a man's dumb blunders. In fact if you do these things on a consistent basis you may even get away with blue murder. So, it's worth a little time learning.

Give them money

If your partner is not working it would probably be a good idea to give her some money. Not only will it make her feel loved, but, believe it or not, it is part of being romantic along with all the other things you do. Let's be frank, you like sex don't you? Then please do these romantic things (actually, the more money you give the better, but just make sure you can first handle sex 24 hrs a day, first). You see, it's all part of love making, and if you think that sex just starts in the bedroom, you are not just dumb, you're dumber, and need to read more books. For those who don't have a lot of money or are very tight with money, the amount you give her does not have to be huge. But what about SOME (very dumb men don't give any, and their wives have to ask like a child). If you don't like to waste money, you need to think of it as investing in your relationship, and consider how much money you will lose if the marriage ends up in divorce. Let them spend the money how they want because that way it will make them feel even more loved (knowing woman, they will spend it on you, the family and things for the house anyway!). Ask marriage counsellors, and they will probably say that men who don't give their wives personal money tend to also stifle and overly control their wives in other areas (other than the subtle controlling effect of properly directed love). Consequently, instead of making a woman feel loved, the opposite happens, and the relationship ends up on the rocks. It's about that simple. Of course you can choose your own destiny, but why take the road that leads to suffering for both yourself and others around you. It makes no sense at all.

Some things to avoid

You don't make a woman feel loved by:

a) Putting her down.

b) Complaining to her about everything she does wrong.

c) Being overly critical.

d) Making her feel dumb.

e) Treating or talking to her like a child, or talking to her in a condescending way.

f) Making all the decisions for her, and not allowing her to express her individualism.

g) Continually threatening her.

h) Losing your temper with her.

i) Walking away when she is upset or crying – she needs you to listen, to be understanding and consoling.

j) Going down the pub with the boys when she is premenstrual (actually the time she needs your love the most). It's not the best time men.

PRETTY POODLE AND PIT BULL DIFFERENCES

Chapter 4

How women differ from men

Sometimes, I think some men differ from their female partner about as much as a Pit bull differs from a pretty Poodle. When Pit bulls start to think a Poodle is another Pit bull there could well be problems, and the same is true when men think women are like men.

Unfortunately, one of the biggest problems in male/female relationships is a lack of understanding on the part of men concerning the extent to which males and females differ. Now I can hear some men already saying, "I know, I know!"

Well, many of those men, who say that, don't know the extent to which women differ from men because saying those words is often a sign that they don't listen – especially to their wives. As a result, they often treat their wives like they would other men, and to their bewilderment experience negative reactions. As I have mentioned previously, it's a bit like someone, who doesn't know much about computers, pressing the wrong buttons, and then wondering what they did wrong.

Having stated the above, I need to qualify that it's my view, from experience and observation, that men and women are not totally different. Of course, there are women who act like men and men who act like women. And some men are gay. However, the belief of many writers and researchers over the years is that, on average, women are sufficiently different from men physically, emotionally, academically, psychologically and spiritually to warrant writing books about the subject. So with that in mind, I will now share my experience, study and conclusions about these differences. Some of the points I make are quite simple, but I feel the need to make them because they seem to get lost in the back of men's minds instead of being more toward the front, where the knowledge can be put to good use. But before I do that, I would briefly like to mention a few scientific studies that have been done, concerning how a woman's brain differs from a man's, to give credence to observed mental differences.

Scientific studies comparing male/female brains

Since the 1990s scientists have had the ability to scan the brain using different techniques like MRI scanning. In 1995 at Yale University a team of scientists led by Drs Bennet and Shaywitz conducted tests on 19 men and 19 women. Using MIR to detect minor changes to blood flow to different parts of the brain, they confirmed that men used mainly the left brain for speech tasks, while women used both left and right regions.

In another study in 2002, Israeli researchers from The Chaim Sheba Medical Centre in Israel examined male and female brains, and found distinct differences in the developing fetus after 26 weeks of pregnancy. The disparities could be seen when using an ultrasound scanner. The corpus callosum, the bridge of nerve tissue that connects the right and left sides of the brain, had a thicker measurement in female fetuses than in male fetuses. Observations of adult brains show that this area may remain larger in females. "Females seem to have language functioning in both sides of the brain," says Martha Bridge Denckla, PhD, a research scientist at Kennedy Krieger Institute.

In a new brain connectivity study from Penn Medicine, published in the *Proceedings of the National Academy of Sciences*, they found striking differences in the neural wiring of men and women that's lending credence to some commonly held beliefs about their behaviour. In an article published by Pen Medicine in December 2, 2013 it was reported that Ragini Verma, PhD, researcher at the University of Pennsylvania, together with an associate professor and other colleagues – found that maps of neural circuitry showed, on average, women's brains were highly connected across the left and right hemispheres – in contrast to men's brains, where the connections were typically larger between the front and back regions. The greatest surprise was how much the findings supported old stereotypes, with men's brains apparently wired more for perception and co-ordinated actions, and women's more for social skills and memory, making them better equipped for multitasking.

Regarding another aspect of the brain, according to Encyclopedia Britannica, the hippocampus, which is located in the inner (medial) region of the temporal lobe, forms part of the limbic system, and is particularly important in producing emotion. Wikipedia says that studies have shown that activation of the hippocampus is more dominant on the left side of hippocampus in females, while it is more dominant on the right side in males. This in turn influences cognitive reasoning; women use more verbal strategies than men when performing a task that requires cognitive thinking (to do with processing information).

Having given you a few examples of scientific studies that have been conducted concerning male and female brain differences, I would now like to give you my own observations that I have gathered over a forty year period. Some points I make might be very simple, but you would be amazed at how many men (with thicker blockheads I guess) either ignore them or are just plain ignorant – either that, or they are just past caring, and have chosen to adopt more of a careless, blunt meat axe approach toward the opposite sex for one reason or another. That's YOU? "Oh, sorry I apologize" – please feel free to tear this book up.

My observations

Some of the following observations (with a bit of humour and exaggeration added) you may consider to be a bit DOG-matic and my opinion only, while others you may be able to easily relate to. I hope by sharing my thoughts on the matter you will at least see if anything fits your female partner, and as a result, enable you to treat her with more understanding – and not like you would another bloke (man) or like a Pit bull would treat a kitten, so to speak.

See below a list of generalisations, and, yes, there are women who don't fit the general characteristics – probably, in some cases, women with lower proportions of 0estrogen (female hormone) or bigger doses of Testosterone (male hormone). Some of the points below will be expanded on in other chapters.

Exaggerated gender differences

Women like to vent their feelings, because they feel better afterwards – so let them. Men like to chill out and watch TV.

Women are consoling. Men tell women to pull themselves together (big mistake).

Women are feeling creatures, and wonder if men have got any.

Women are sensitive – men are blockheads.

Women tend not to stay long on the same subject – men have one track minds, and it's not always on sex ladies.

Women have an eye for detail – men are blind.

Women are soft physically and emotionally – women think men are mean.

Women have wider eye vision. It's a scientific fact. You don't know it men, but they can see you looking at them. So be careful.

Women are good at finding things – men are good at losing things, especially if they get side tracked.

Women don't appreciate it when men generalise, and will come up with the exceptions, even if a man qualifies his statement

Women are more sensitive to touch because of thinner skin – men are thick as bricks.

Women like multitasking – men like concentrating on one thing at a time, and turn off the TV when someone phones them.

Women sometimes need a shoulder to lean on – sometimes men like women leaning on them, and it makes them feel good.

Women get scarred – men pretend not to be.

Women are cautious drivers – some idiot men get angry at them on the road, but of course that's not you huh!

Women tell white lies because they have soft natures. Men are blunt.

Women gossip (oops! Did I say that? Surely I'm a blockhead, anyway my wife told me they do that at her work) – Men can't talk.

Women react emotionally – men are too scared to.

Women fall to pieces in emergency situations – men quickly sort out what's what, and do what is needed.

Women lack confidence – men act macho.

Women can be bitchy – men make women bitchy.

Women are sweet (thought I better quickly mention that here, after my last comment, mmm!).

Women get easily hurt – so get your big hoof off their toes when you dance with them, okay!

Women are gentle, but be careful men because there are some "toughies" out there, and others that are good at hitting below the belt if you don't treat them right – ouch!

Women like cuddles – men like sex.

Women are sometimes just satisfied with a cuddle – men like sex.

Women are good homemakers. Leave them alone men. I've seen too many bachelor pads.

Women change their minds – men cause them to.

Little things are important to women – men wonder what the fuss is about.

Women are good at keeping busy – men sit. Some women call them couch potatoes.

Women are like busy worker bees, men are like drones – in more ways than one. Think about it.

Women like people. It doesn't matter if the people are, fat, ugly, or disabled – men like cars, things and football.

Women are good at talking – men grunt sometimes.

Women like pretty things – I once lived with a guy who painted the rooms of his house dark brown. He was single.

Women love sweet compliments. Actually they thrive on them – some men know that only too well.

Women are beauty conscious – men can get dressed in 5 minutes flat.

Women like to be organised and prepared – men say, "let's go".

Women do not have the best sense of priority – this often leaves men bewildered.

Women are clean – men are dirty, and don't see dust.

Women smell nice – blockheads just smell, and then try to pull women into them on the dance floor.

Women go silent when they are upset or angry – men go silent when they're thinking about something, thinking about nothing, or just got nothing to say.

Women need to be comforted when they are sick – men want to be left alone.

Women like to help – men sometimes think women are being bossy, when they are just trying to help.

Women panic – men like to look cool and in control, even if they're not.

Women like romance – men play the game.

Women like dancing – men play the game.

Women like dancing with each other – men don't mind dancing in a mixed group of males and females, but don't ever ask men if they would like to dance with each other.

Women love going to the toilet together – men can't understand a women's fascination with the place.

Women have low self-esteem – men with no job or money feel the same.

Women are soft physically – men are just plain tough, eh men!

Women tend to be soft and inconsistent with discipline – some men today are like women.

Women like men who are hard to get – men don't like women who play hard to get.

Women are moody, especially once a month – men start to get more moody later in life when they run out of testosterone (male hormone).

Women are easily shattered like glass – men are clumsy and as thick as bricks.

Women are loving – men have tough love, or are just plain blockheads.

Women cry easily – men cry about serious issues, but never over a traffic infringement.

Women like romantic movies – men hate them.

Women are sentimental – men are blockheads.

Women's love is conditional (they are sensitive to how men treat them) – some men get worn down after years, and run out of unconditional love.

Women are swayed by charming words – some men take advantage of them.

Women love a deep voice, and could listen to it all day. A woman's voice can be so sweet.

Women like intimacy – men don't know what that is.

Women like to be connected – men don't know what that is.

Women are affectionate to each other – men feel uncomfortable if another man intrudes in his personal zone. And they are horrified if a "girl" they take out turns out to be gay.

Women are sensitive, and men's negative expressions and ill-chosen words can upset them.

Women believe easily, and salesman like them – men get angry with their wives for over-spending.

Women don't understand men – especially when men chill out, just sit, or do and say nothing. One comedian described this as a man opening his empty box.

Women are picky – men have too many faults to feel like being picky.

Women are friendly – men are silent introverts.

Women are not so good at maths – there have been studies about that.

Women are not good navigators – according to scientific studies, women's brains are wired differently to men's brains.

Women are subjective.

Women like money and going shopping – men like sex.

Women like to improve the house – some men can live in a pigsty.

Women need to feel secure.

Women are indirect – men are blunt. Some women say men are too blunt.

Women beat around the bush – men are blunt and to the point. If you don't believe me, just look at some of the previous points I have made.

Women are not good under pressure, and at handling stress – men sometimes find it difficult, but keep it too themselves.

Women often multitask – men have one track minds.

Women are good at picking up body language – men just like looking at female bodies.

Women don't always know why they feel the way they do – men think women don't always know why they feel the way they do.

Women are not logical – men are logical except when they think about sex.

Women like strong leaders – men pretend to be that way.

Women are interested in relationships – men are interested in things and the football.

Women find it hard to be firm – men find it hard to be too soft.

Women twist what men say – men are bewildered when women twist what they say.

Women don't hit harder, but hit lower. They believe you are not easy to hurt because you are a man.

Women hit below the belt to make a man feel the hurt the man just inflicted on them.

Women are not so good at decision making if given many choices – men often make bad decisions, but are quick to make them.

Women like to take their time shopping – men prefer to sit and do nothing or have a coffee. They also hate following behind a woman when she shops.

Women put more importance on their wedding than men do – men put more importance on life after the marriage than the wedding.

Women need understanding from men – men don't know what they really mean.

Women need a hug – men don't always recognise when they need one.

Women like time to prepare – men are good at springing things on their wives at the last moment.

Women are not the best at prioritising, and get bogged down with detail.

Women need to take their time dressing up to go out, especially if it's a formal occasion.

Women like a man who knows what he is doing and where he is going, rather than a man who is uncertain.

Women often get bored when a man gets too deep about a particular subject, and stays on it too long.

Since women are so good at detail, they are a great help to men. Whereas men tend to focus on main or overall issues, and often overlook detail.

Having now spoken in generalities about many of the differences between men and women, with a bit of exaggeration to illustrate the point, the next chapter goes into more detail about some of those differences, and suggests ways for men to treat women like ladies and less like blokes (men).

DON'T TREAT A CAT LIKE A DOG

Chapter 5

Don't treat a woman like a bloke (man)

How would you like your female partner to purr with contentment and happiness, just like a little kitten? Well, if that sounds good to you, make sure you stop barking and treating her like a dog. Otherwise, instead of purring, she may end up giving you a few scratches. Having read the previous chapter, hopefully you have an appreciation of the many differences between men and women. Due to ignorance of those differences, a man often makes the mistake of treating a woman like he does another bloke. A woman is simply a different creation, and it can be very beneficial to male/female relationships if a man understands that a woman has different needs to his.

One of the greatest causes of conflict between people is when individual needs, likes or desires are not fulfilled. A woman's needs should not be dismissed as unimportant nor be invalidated by men. Rather, they should be understood, and if possible fulfilled. It is important that men try and look at things from their female partner's perspective in addition to their own.

In this chapter, I make a number of points about women and give some advice. It's my belief that a lack of understanding and application of the helpful points I make in this chapter add up to mean one thing to a woman – that her partner doesn't love her. Actually, the truth may be that he does love her – BUT treats her like a bloke instead of like a woman because of ignorance. Now, I'm sure that most of you men don't really want to marry a bloke, so it may not be such a bad idea to take time out from TV, football, cars, business, etc, and give the subject a bit of thought from time to time. No, you don't have to suddenly apply everything all at once like a bull at a gate, and suddenly become someone else. That subject is covered in a later chapter entitled "Don't be Mr Plastic". Rather, I suggest that you just let some of the points I'm going to cover gradually penetrate into your subconscious with the aim of adjusting the way you treat your female partner over time. When you begin to experience some good results, hopefully, applying some of the advice will become more a part of you and will be easier to do. With that in mind, I will now pass on some of my personal experience/suggestions and what I've learnt from my own reading and study about relationships over the past 40 years. Hope it helps.

Don't rush her

One mistake a man sometimes makes is to ask a woman to go somewhere without giving her enough time to prepare. Some men don't seem to understand that a woman likes to be organised, prepared, think in detail, is beauty conscious and that small things are important to her. The problem is that a man too often asks his partner to go somewhere at the last moment, after having had plenty of prior opportunity to do so. Not only does this cause her stress, but it also conveys that you don't really think about her (love her) or appreciate her needs. Of course, it depends on the occasion, and sometimes spontaneity is fine. However on other occasions (especially formal ones) a woman needs more advanced notice. You may be able to get away with last minute notice with men, but you'd better not try it on a woman unless you want to put her in a bad mood or be sent to the doghouse for a brief spell.

Before going out, women generally need more time than men to do things such as: their hair, makeup, nails, etc – and depending on the occasion, they may need time to prepare food, tidy the house and do other similar kind of things. Even things like: having a shower, cleaning their teeth and dressing themselves seems to take them longer. Furthermore, because they are usually the main house keeper, they have ten times more to do than you do before they are ready to go somewhere.

So the best advice I can give you is to plan ahead, notify them in advance, and thus avoid rushing them.

A man should let a woman release her feelings

One of the most valuable principles I ever learned, concerning male/ female relationships, is that a man should let a woman release her feelings. This is a general principle, and of course does not necessarily apply in every situation. However, it does apply in MANY situations, and I personally have employed it over the years to great effect. In defining this principle, I have been very careful to use the word 'release' instead of the word 'express'. The reason I chose this word is because a woman can express her feelings, but unless she feels listened to or understood by her male partner, she may feel like she is talking to a brick wall. Subsequently, even though she expresses her feelings, she doesn't really get to release them. In other words, get rid of them so she can feel better and think about something positive. This principle of a man letting a woman release her feelings is not exactly new, and has been mentioned in many books about relationships – only it has been explained by others using different terms. The first time I saw the principle mentioned was in a book entitled "Men are from Mars Women are from Venus" by John Gray. Even though it is a well known principle among those who have written books about male/ female relationships, it is so important to know that I had to include it in this book. However, I have put a slightly different spin on the subject by saying that a woman needs to "release" or get rid of feelings, rather than saying a woman needs to "express" her feelings.

Now, there are many different occasions when a woman needs to release her feelings. For example, she may have had a difficult time with her children. She may have had problems with a relationship at work. She may be feeling stressed or experiencing premenstrual tension. One of the ways a woman gets rid of these feelings, so she can feel better, is to share them with somebody who will just listen and be understanding. Now of course, I am not saying that a woman is totally different from a man, and sometimes a man does the same thing. However, in a lot of situations a man chooses to get rid of feelings in a different way. For example, if a man has had a stressful day at work, instead of talking about his problems, often he deals with them by trying to forget about them. He does this by doing things like watching the football and reading the paper. On other occasions, he might do things such as: go outside for a smoke, lie on the bed, chill out and do nothing for a while. Or, sometimes he might just quietly think out the problem to himself, and does not really want to talk about it with someone else – especially if he feels his partner would not really understand the situation. Some books describe this behaviour as a man going into his cave to be alone for a while. Talking about feelings with his partner, or for that matter other men, does not appear as needful for a man as it is for a woman. A woman seems to talk about her feelings quite often, particularly with other females.

Getting back to the subject, there are at least five different things a man does which prevents a woman from fulfilling her need to release her feelings. They are as follows, and are explained in more detail further in this chapter:

1) Offer solutions
2) Invalidate her feelings
3) Tell her to pull herself together
4) Go brain dead
5) Walk away

Offer solutions

One of the most natural things for a man to do, when a woman expresses her feelings about problems she has had during the day, is to try and solve her problems by providing solutions. However, often this is a mistake, complicates the situation and causes her to have additional negative feelings. It also interrupts her, and doesn't allow her to empty her feelings. You see, often, when a woman expresses her feelings, she is simply wanting to get rid of them by sharing them with someone who will listen with empathy and understanding. Often, she is not looking for solutions, and usually does not ask a man to provide one. Despite a man's best intentions, chances are that the best thing he can do is allow her to release her feelings, and thus get rid of them so she can feel and cope better.

I remember on one occasion a woman telling me on Facebook all about the problems she was having with her husband. When she began to express herself about the problems she was having, I immediately recognised that what she needed was someone to just listen and not interrupt. Especially, not interrupt with all kinds of advice. So instead of interrupting, I responded briefly using such words as: "oh really", "yes I see", "yeah I understand what you mean" or "that must be hard" etc. It worked like a dream. She poured out her feelings for about half an hour, and then ran out of steam. She felt much better after, and thanked me for taking an interest. I believe she just needed someone to talk with, which helped her to cope with what was a pretty unsolvable problem.

I also remember, on another occasion, interviewing a man who was interested in my Filipino Penwriting Club. He told me how his female partner once vented her anger towards him. Apparently, instead of justifying and defending himself, he just listened. She eventually got rid of her feelings, and he gave her a big hug. It worked wonderfully, and she changed from being angry to showering him with love and affection.

I also remember a lady I know telling me about an occasion when she was having a really lousy day. She had to pick up a hire car she had ordered only to find, apparently, that it was not ready because they had made a mistake. Well, that was the final straw, and so she let loose and blasted the man at the car hire place. By doing that, she was able to release all of the negative feelings she had been keeping bottled up all day. The fact that he was the service provider and she was the customer meant he probably just let her do it. After getting rid of her feelings, she said she felt really great for the rest of the day. The moral of the story is that sometimes a woman may use an excuse to release all her feelings on a man, however, regardless of the rights or wrongs of the matter, it's probably best to let her do it so she can feel better. Therefore, a very useful principle for a man to apply in his relationships with a woman in various situations is: A man needs to let a woman release her feelings by listening, not interrupting or offering solutions.

Invalidate her feelings

Another thing a man does when a woman wants to unload her feelings is to invalidate them. In other words, make her feel that she has no valid reason to have such feelings. For example, he may say something like, "What are you getting all upset about?" "What's the big problem?" "Why are you worried about small things?" Or he may invalidate her feelings by simply brushing them off as though they were not important or trivial. By doing this, he sends a message to his female partner that she has no right to have those feelings, and that he is not interested in hearing them expressed. Consequently, a woman does not get the opportunity to release those feelings, and get rid of them in the way she needs, which would have helped her to cope and given her some emotional stability.

Tells her to pull herself together

A third thing a man does that prevents a woman from releasing her feelings is to try and force her to STOP her feelings. By doing this he is treating her like a man. He does this by saying things like: "snap out of it", "pull yourself together". In many cases this is exactly the opposite of what a woman needs to do. It goes totally against the flow. In general, women have a greater need to get these feelings out, compared to men, and so expectations from men should be different.

Goes brain dead

Sometimes, when a woman suddenly vents her feelings in anger at a man it takes him by surprise, and he doesn't really know what to do. This is particularly true when her anger just appears out of nowhere. Often, instead of reacting, a man is just stunned, and looks at his wife with a blank expression on his face. It's like he has gone brain dead. The reason for this is because he thinks to himself: "if I say something she is going to react", "and if I don't say something she is going to react". It's what is called a catch twenty two situation, and he feels damned if he does and damned if he doesn't. What he really needs to do is not look brain dead, but at least grunt or make some sort of noise to show that he is listening and that she is not talking to a brick wall – thus allowing for her need to release her feelings.

Walk away

Last but not least, when a woman starts releasing all her feelings on a man, he may simply walk away. Now, I know there are times when a man feels he needs to do so, but he should think carefully first. The reason he should think first is because walking away often prevents a woman from getting rid of those feelings and only adds feelings of rejection – making her feel that you don't care about her. It's like you're saying, I'm not interested in how you feel – STOP your feelings. Yes men, I know in some cases you may need a bit of a break and to go outside or into your cave for a while (like the shed where there are a few cold beers), but you need to be careful not to make her feel that you don't love her. You may need to give her a bit of time to get rid of some of those feelings. And if she's crying, she may need a hug and a kiss. After that, you may go to your cave. It's got to be better than the doghouse.

Women are easily hurt

When I was a young man, as I was sitting in a lecture for singles about male/female relationships, I heard a valuable analogy that I have never forgotten. It went like this: "Women are like glass". They therefore need to be handled with care because they can be easily shattered." In other words, a woman is very sensitive to words and actions. Their feelings can be very easily hurt, and sometimes they can feel deeply wounded emotionally. It's similar to the way a woman can be easily hurt physically by a man, if he is too rough. Negative words hurt their feelings more easily than they do men, in general, and abusive words shatter. It's like the difference between a man hitting another man in the stomach and a man hitting a woman in the stomach. The man that was hit may stager to his feet, but a woman will probably just buckle in pain and not be able to get up for some time. This kind of thing is also commonly called 'verbal abuse', and is a legitimate reason why some women find shelter in female refuge centres.

Rather than be abused verbally, a woman needs to be handled with gentleness, understanding and care. You may be able to get away with rough talk and thoughtless actions toward another bloke, but please don't try it on a woman (unless you are a masochist of course). Men need to be particularly thoughtful about the words they choose when talking to a woman because using the wrong word can be hurtful – and will be discussed further under the next subheading.

Sometimes, a man mistreats a woman by losing his temper, swearing, abusing her and resorting to name calling. This topic will also be covered further in another chapter, but suffice to say here that this type of behaviour is simply divorce material. In fact, one internet site I viewed about this type of subject claimed that they could predict with 95% accuracy that a particular couple would end in divorce – simply by listening to how the couple showed contempt and disrespect for each other in their conversations.

Abusive behaviour shatters a woman like a piece of glass, and she will never forget the hurt for years to come. In fact, it hurts so badly that she will remind you of your words years later as part of future arguments – adding more complications to your relationship. Those words are poison, and should be avoided like the plague. The same goes for physical abuse, which is ten times worse. Please men, don't do either.

So, the lesson is: Men be gentle. A woman is like a piece of glass, and needs to be handled with care.

Be careful with your use of words

Another thing a man needs to be careful about, when communicating to a woman, is his choice of words – words that may be perceived to be offensive. They are also described as words that have negative connotations. A man may not actually mean to be offensive or hurt a woman's feelings, but choosing the wrong word can have that effect. Yes, all women are different, and the way they react sometimes depends on how they have been treated by men in the past and what scars they still have, but it's a good principle to keep in mind. The bottom line is that it's not always a good idea to use the same words to communicate to a woman as you would use to communicate to a man, if you want to avoid offence and conflict. The concept, that a man needs to be careful with the words he uses, when communicating to a woman, was confirmed by some experiences I had when testing some of the content of this book. For example, I remember on one occasion talking about the contents of my book with some of my female relatives, when I got a negative reaction because of a word I used. It was then that I learnt it would be better NOT to use the word *'deal'*, when talking about how a man should treat a woman. For example, rather than say that the book is about *dealing* with women, which was perceived as a negative comment or a put down, it was better and less offensive to say that the book was about men *'treating'* women in a better way. Some refer to the right choice of words as political correctness.

Another word in the book I chose to swap for the word *'emotional'*, in reference to women, was the word *'feeling'*. In other words, instead of saying that women are *'emotional'*, I found it is safer and less offensive to describe women as feeling people. The reason this may be a better word to use is because a man often uses the word *'emotional'*, to put a woman down or speak about her in a negative way. I also read a book written by a woman about what women wish men knew about them – and noticed she (the author) liked to use the word *'feeling'* instead of the word *'emotional'* in reference to women. Using the word *'emotional'* carries the risk of being perceived by a woman to be an expression of a negative attitude from a man. No, a woman should not really make a man feel like he is walking on eggshells, but being more aware of using the right words, and learning over time to use those words, as a matter of habit, can be helpful with relationships and make them less complicated. This subject became very pronounced in my mind when I was testing what title to give this book. Whatever the title, I thought it needed to grab people's attention and have a bit of punch about it. I had thought of several ideas until a friend of mine, who has a good sense of humour, came up with a title that in some respects seemed to fit the bill. I can't remember his exact words, but he said something like this: why don't you call the book "How to prevent a Sweet Wife from turning into a Nasty Bitch". I then added the words – for Beginners and Blockheads. I later decided to change a few words and thought I might call the book: "How to Stop 'turning' a Sweet Lady into a Nasty Bitch", and thus direct more of the blame on certain men (mainly blockheads). To me, it was a bit safer because it directed attention more to the audience I intended to target – men. At the time, it came across to me as a humorous type of title, and certainly had the ability to grab people's attention. However, I must admit that I was concerned about the use of the word *'bitch'*.

Later on, I showed the suggested title to another female friend, and to my surprise she said it was great. It surprised me because she did not seem to be offended. In retrospect, I have since realised that to a large extent she had been protected from bad treatment from men, and did not carry many emotional scars that many women do today. She also said that men had always treated her well. In fact she even seemed to like them. The fact that she came from the country and belonged to a close knit church group, which she joined as a teenager, may have helped her to hold such an opinion. However, at the time, her comment gave me a little confidence about the title, and I thought women would just see the title as a joke and be curious to pick the book up and read it.

On another occasion, I took the title along to a book club, consisting of men and woman, and handed it around to see their reaction. But before doing that, I mentioned the title to one of the ladies, and observed her immediate reaction was to laugh. Once again, it seemed to confirm that most ladies would just take it as a joke, and be interested to see what was inside. However, after passing the title around to the members of the book club and discussing the title, I focussed their attention on the use of the word *bitch* on the front cover. When I focussed on that word, they seemed to get bogged down with it and its negative connotations to the point that the unanimous opinion was that I should scrap the title because it was too offensive.

This negative view about the use of the word *'bitch'* was later confirmed by a group of my relatives, with varying degrees of diplomacy, ranging from silence, to polite suggestion, to "choose another title", to out-rightly saying that they hated the title. They simply did not like the use of that word bitch. I later quizzed one of the ladies to find out why she hated the word so much. She then told me about some of the negative experiences she had with men in the work place, ranging from bullying, being put down to verbal abuse. It was then I realised that this is the case with a lot of women, and that using the word *'bitch'*, does not go down well because of its negative connotations. However, I did notice, interestingly, that none of my lady relatives had a problem with the word blockhead, which was also in the title. In fact, one of them even suggested that I call the book "Blockhead Guide to Better Marriage". I have since noticed that not many men are offended by that term. I believe, this indicates a difference in sensitivity between men and women. Eventually, one of my sisters suggested I change the title to "How to stay out of the Doghouse". Hence, how the title of the book came about. Subsequently, to be safe, I thought I had better change the title to the one my sister suggested rather run the risk of being sent to the doghouse by the thousands of women readers.

Don't be blunt or too open

Honesty is a virtue, but being too open and blunt is not recommended in a lot of circumstances, when it comes to a relationship with a woman. This may sound rather strange to some, and most women would probably say they like an open and honest relationship – but do they really? I'm not suggesting telling them lies (even though I believe there is a song out by a woman singer that went something like this: "tell me lies, tell me lies, tell me sweet little lies"), but sometimes the raw truth can really hurt them. What woman, for example, wants a man to come straight out and say she is fat and needs to lose weight? What woman wants to hear a man say she looks silly in the new dress she bought, or that the meal she made him tasted yuk? I once knew a man who was like that, and even though you could rely on him to tell the truth he certainly would not sugar coat things he said. While this was not such a problem in his relationships with men, believe me, it was a problem with his relationships with women. In short, he made them feel anything from embarrassed, inadequate and discouraged to outright furious. I thought if he ever got married he would have a few problems, and sure enough it came true. He is still married. Hopefully he has been learning fast, and has had a few rough edges knocked off his personality.

A man needs to be particularly careful about commenting on the food his wife or partner prepares for him. The reason for this is because if you say you don't like it you run the risk that she will take it personally, and feel that you don't appreciate her as a person or her efforts to please you. If you're not careful she may end up saying: "make your own food then." and storm off in a huff. It's a bit like when a man does a lot of hard work trying to improve the house at his wife's request, only to find she doesn't like his work and suggests he pull it all down and get someone else to do it. It's not easy to take.

In conclusion, the lesson for men is: don't be too blunt, and be careful with a woman's feelings.

ROTTWEILER GUIDE TO LOVE AND SEX

Chapter 6

JWG

Three mysteries about Sex Explained

Just before you next pounce at your partner like a hungry Rottweiler, I need to explain a few things about kitty-cats. Further to the previous chapter, another way a woman differs from a man concerns the subject of SEX. In this chapter, I would like to explain a number of mysteries concerning sex that a man needs to be aware of. By mysteries, I mean mysteries to Rottweilers and Pit bulls – not kittens

The first mystery

Why do some women say they don't want or need sex? This book would not be complete unless I explained this great mystery to men. Over the years, I've heard a number of women say they don't want or need sex, and to a lot of men this statement does not make much sense. By the way, I'm not referring to when women say they don't want sex because they have got a headache. I mean when they just say, during the course of a normal conversation, that they don't want or need sex. To a man, it seems that they don't LIKE sex, but that's not what they mean either. They actually do like sex, but say they don't want it or need it. So men, are you CONFUSED? Well, let me continue to explain a few more differences between men and women that men need to understand – this time concerning sex.

Firstly, when a woman says she doesn't want or need sex, she is NOT saying that she doesn't like the pleasure involved with sex. She DOES. What she often really means is that she doesn't like LOVELESS sex. A selfish type of sex that makes her feel like an object – that she is only being used to satisfy a man's sexual gratification. In other words, two minute, wham bam, thank you ma'am, type of sex that makes a woman feel like a blow up doll, rather than a human being with feelings that are being cared about. In fact, some women don't like men using the word sex at all, but prefer the subject to be referred to as love making. Putting it another way, a woman likes LOVING sex, not SELFISH one sided sex. So don't get the wrong idea when she says she doesn't want or need sex, because she does want and need the type of sex where the husband really cares for her pleasure as well as his own. She prefers sex with a man who is loving and does all the little things that makes her FEEL loved. This includes being understanding of her needs by being gentle, kind, patient, and includes kissing, cuddling, patting, petting, stroking, sweet words and foreplay etc. So men, when you hear women say they don't want or need sex, I hope you will now know what they mean. They just mean they want LOVING sex, not SELFISH sex. They need to feel truly loved, cared about and not just used.

For a woman love and sex are not separate

In general, a woman finds it difficult to separate love from the act of sex. In other words, to her it's one subject – love making. In contrast, a man has no difficulty in separating love from sex. He can either enjoy sex without being in love with somebody or enjoy sex with someone who he is "in love" with and cares about. This difference can be a real trap for a woman who jumps into bed with a man too soon, without testing whether the man really loves her, and wants to commit himself in a long term relationship, such as marriage. A woman sometimes believes that if a man has sex with her it must be an expression of his love. However, in some cases, a man may be just taking advantage of her, and be enjoying the pleasure of having sex with someone he finds sexually attractive. He may not really be in love or want a long term relationship. In other cases, the man may really love a lady and want loving sex, like she does. As general rule, a woman has sex with a man for one of two reasons. She has sex because she loves the man, or some have sex in exchange for money from the man. The latter is called prostitution and is one of the oldest professions in the world. Usually, both parties are happy for the exchange. However, it is extremely rare that a woman pays a man for sex. This once again demonstrates how men and woman are different. The fact that men are willing to pay money for sex with someone they have never met before, shows how they can separate sex from love and enjoy sex without love – whereas, a woman is generally not interested in doing that, and wants only loving sex or money.

Don't be too direct

One very good attribute that a man has is the ability to be blunt and get to the point. You may have been noticing that about me, while you have been reading this chapter. However, please don't try this when it comes to having sex with a woman. Actually, a man should be careful with this approach in general, regarding all aspects of relationships with a woman. While this book is not intended to cover in detail techniques regarding having sex with a woman (other books do that), there is one basic thing that I need to mention – and that is: a man needs to allow time for his wife/ female partner to become aroused by indirect foreplay before she will be ready for the act of sex. In the area of arousal, there is a basic difference between men and women that now needs to be explained.

Where does sex begin for a woman?

If I was to ask a man where sex begins he might say: "in the bedroom of course". However, for a woman, sex, which she would rather call 'love making', begins well outside of the bedroom. In other words, part of the foreplay involved in the act of sex is not just physical, but a matter of how a man treats and loves his partner on a day to day basis. If she does not FEEL loved outside the bedroom, which has already been covered in an earlier chapter, it may also affect sex in the bedroom. Sex will either be not as good for her or you – or there will simply be NONE. A good sex life does not come cheap and depends a lot on how a woman is loved throughout each day. Apart from that, she needs plenty of time (usually about 20 to 30 minutes of gentle foreplay) before the final act of sex. But please, don't start looking at your watch.

One marriage counsellor put it this way:

Women love sex, but differently than men do. Women love sex that comes as a result of feeling loved, while for a man desire is far more sight-stimulated. A man might even want his partner sexually even in a bad marriage. Women are more driven to sex when communication levels are high and she feels her words and feelings (and thus herself) are valued. For women, emotional and sexual intimacy is developed outside the bedroom. If the relationship feels neglected in the other areas of the house she will not want to have fun with you inside the bedroom. Women need to talk and be listened to about all the areas of their life no matter how mundane you perceive them. When we do our training Marriage Skills for Police Marriages we tell men, if you want good sex, give good communication. If the communication is not there, women's libidos go down and they often report they do not enjoy or desire sexual encounters with their man. So be a good boy, or you may find yourself going thirsty.

Other reasons women say they don't want sex

Below is a list of other reasons why women say or indicate they don't want to have sex:

1) They are under stress, whether it is as a result of their occupation, house work, looking after kids or financial situation.
2) They are tired
3) They are too busy

4) They have a headache – literally.
5) They have just had a baby – and are preoccupied with him or her.
6) Their sex drive is not as high when they are older and have had a few babies.
7) They have a hormonal problem.
8) They are in a bad marriage.

Twenty ways to guarantee a sex free marriage

Below is a list of twenty ways to turn a woman off and guarantee your marriage is sex free. Yes, I'm joking, but I hope you get the drift:

1) Make love with smokers breath
2) Smell of BO
3) Jump into bed drunk
4) Tell your wife about the time you had at the strip club.
5) Tell your wife that she needs to lose weight
6) Spend more time down the pub than with your partner
7) Never show any of your feelings
8) Forget her birthday and your wedding anniversary
9) Be a couch potato, leave her all the work, don't help with the kids and leave all responsibility to her.
10) Think only of yourself.
11) Push her away, when she wants a cuddle
12) Never cuddle her outside of the bedroom
13) Act too desperate for sex.
14) Make her feel like she is your mother
15) Have two minute sex like a Rottweiler

16) Cater to her every whim
17) Act like you're hard as nails, like you got no feelings or compassion
18) Complain about everything she does
19) Make her feel unappreciated
20) Be thoughtless and inconsiderate

More detail a man needs to know

1) Affection without sex.

Touch is very important to a woman, but if she feels that the only time you touch her or give her a hug is when you want sex, she may begin to not touch you or be unwilling to receive your touch and affection. Most women like affection, want to hold hands, be massaged, and exchange a few playful slaps etc. But if a woman believes your only purpose for that type of touch is foreplay, she may stop touching YOU because she feels devalued and not loved. So the point to keep in mind is to give her plenty of hugs, kisses, touches etc, apart from the purpose of having sex with her.

2) Don't be too needy

Years ago I went dancing every weekend. Through that experience, I learnt that if there was one thing that a woman withdrew from was a hungry looking sex starved man. It was almost as though a woman had in built radar so she could detect such a man from a mile away. Usually, when such a man asked a woman to dance, to his bewilderment, the answer was usually NO. Now things are a bit different when a man is married to a woman, and sometimes a bit of passion is good. However, if the man seems to be always like a panting puppy dog looking for his reward, it may come across as weakness. And, generally, it's been my experience that women are more attracted to strength. Now, I know all situations are different, and sometimes for one reason or another a man may not be getting enough sex from his partner. So, far be it for me to advise you in this matter, and you will have to work that one out for yourselves – except to say that some men end up relieving themselves or ask their wives to do it for them if they find that she's not in a sexy mood.

The second sex mystery

The second mystery about sex is that it pictures the way a man should go about, in general, achieving a harmonious relationship with his female partner. Let me explain. An ideal harmonious relationship between a man and his partner is a bit like the sexual union when two people are literally joined as one body. In other words, when a couple are in real harmony with each other it is like they are one body or one person – and the sexual union pictures this ideal perfectly. My personal belief is that God purposely designed sex with that picture in mind – but not only that, I believe the best method to achieve that harmony is also pictured by a man's foreplay before sex takes place. I will now explain further.

With sex, the man generally has to be the <u>one to start things happening</u>. It starts with how he treats her on a day to day basis, and is then followed by what is called foreplay. It's not good if he is <u>too direct</u> because it will cause pain and rejection from his partner. Rather, it's far better if a man gives a woman time, so she will be ready to be physically joined as one body – joined sexually. Well, the same principle applies when it comes to achieving the goal of a harmonious relationship between a man and a woman – becoming like one person. To bring about anywhere close to this type of intimate relationship, I believe (like with sex) a man needs to be primarily the one to initiate and bring about this type of at one relationship. Also, regarding building a more harmonious relationship with his partner, similar to sex, a man needs to subject a woman to a type of foreplay. In other words, to achieve the goal of a harmonious relationship a man should not be too direct or try to rush things, or it will not work. Instead, he needs to gradually bring about harmony, mostly, by example and by subjecting her to the true definition of LOVE – in contrast to purely self desire. Like in the lead up to sex or lovemaking, to foster a good relationship, he needs to be patient, take his time and should not try to force things. In sex, forcing the issue causes pain and rejection, instead of pleasure, and I believe the same type of thing happens in relationships between a man and a woman, if the man tries to force things. It will strain the relationship, irritate the woman and provoke rejection. This is one of the reasons I have a whole chapter entitled: "The buck stops with you, big dog", and firmly believe it is the natural order of things for a man to take the responsibility, regarding the development of a harmonious relationship between him and his female partner.

The third mystery of sex

The next little mystery, regarding sex, I felt was too important to leave out of this book. Actually, it's something that I first discovered by reading another book, which was specifically about the subject of sex, and it certainly made a lot of sense to me. The mystery is: 'unlike a man, a woman does not always need to have an orgasm. In other words, at certain times of the month, it's perfectly ok if a man climaxes first, before she does, and sometimes she may indicate that during the act of sex. This is very important for a man to understand because if he is under the misconception that she, like him, will on every occasion not be satisfied unless she has an orgasm – he may feel pressured, to always try and give her one. She will also sense this, and it may put undue pressure on her to try and fulfil his expectation. Some woman may go as far as faking one.

Now, there are times when a woman really wants to have an orgasm, and this has been mentioned in one book I read as being mainly somewhere in the middle of her cycle, when she is very fertile – as compared to the time in her cycle when she is not fertile. Now, I don't profess to be an expert in the science of all this, but I do know that women have what I call a sweet sexy cycle. It is definitely somewhere in the middle of her full monthly cycle, and when they are most likely to fall pregnant. So it all makes good sense to me. If you want to know more about this subject, I recommend you read "Mars and Venus in the Bedroom" by John Gray.

WOMEN SOMETIMES FEEL CRAZY, BUT DON'T TAKE IT PERSONALLY

Chapter 7

Premenstrual tension

Many men, who are in unhappy marriages or relationships with women, seem to be oblivious, at times, to how their partners are being affected by what is called premenstrual tension – or if they are aware, they don't appear to have much idea how to treat them during that time. It also seems that this topic is not often covered in many books about marriage relationships, yet it is probably one of the most important topics for a man to understand.

Premenstrual Syndrome (PMS) refers to a wide range of physical and emotional symptoms that typically occur about 5 to 11 days before a woman starts her monthly menstrual cycle (when she issues blood). The symptoms vary from woman to woman and may be different from month to month. Some months may be worse than others. These symptoms usually cease when menstruation begins, or shortly thereafter. Furthermore, women suffering from PMS may not experience all the symptoms, and can suffer them with varying degrees of severity.

According to medical sources, physical symptoms may include headaches, cramps, bloating, fatigue, fluid retention, breast tenderness, constipation and diarrhea. Emotional symptoms may include: behavioural changes, eating binges, moodiness and irritability. Some women have mild symptoms; others have symptoms that interfere with work or home life. A few women are completely incapacitated.

As mentioned above, during this time women often become irritable and moody. The reason for this is because the female hormone oestrogen becomes depleted and is at its lowest level. Unfortunately, some men are so out of tune with their partner's feelings that they are often oblivious to the reasons why their female partner behaves differently during this time, and take negative remarks far too personally. Consequently, instead of trying to help their partner cope, they can complicate and inflame the situation. So it's very important that a man knows the best way to respond during what can be a difficult time.

DON'T TAKE IT PERSONALLY

Sometimes, in the course of an argument or conflict during the premenstrual cycle, some ladies may say things that are extremely insulting, and feel like they are going crazy. The degree of craziness they feel is also influenced by their partner's reactions. One lady I know told her husband that sometimes it felt as though she had a gremlin inside of her. At best, ladies say and do things that they normally would not. This situation can be difficult and perplexing for men. However, I have found that a good general rule for men to follow and remember is: DON'T TAKE IT TOO PERSONALLY. All women are different of course, and the way men react to them affects what they do, but their behaviour during this time can range from nit picking, niggly remarks, sarcasm, walking off in a huff, outbursts of anger or going silent to throwing frypans or slapping a man in the face. In extreme cases it can even involve pulling out knives. A woman may even say she hates a man, which may not be true (um – I think, at least, hopefully, not most of the time). In other cases, it has been during that time one of the two people involved has walked out of the relationship.

A lot of a woman's reactions, of course, are affected by what her man has said, done, or not done at that time, and therefore he needs to acknowledge any contribution he has made to the situation. However, to help him avoid taking things too personally, it's very important for him to understand that during menstruation a woman's hormones (oestrogen) are at low levels, and she feels irritable, moody and often finds it's difficult to control her emotional reactions. This is particularly the case when she is experiencing stress (you know men – housework, babies and all that kind of stuff). Consequently, she will have a tendency to take things out on you, and sometimes any excuse will do. Therefore, it helps if a man at least has some idea of what is going on so he can avoid taking it too personally, and making a bigger issue than needs to be. For a man to have zero understanding, tolerance and empathy towards a woman during that time is simply a recipe for disaster.

Here now are a few ideas that I have proven, personally in my own case, to be helpful to employ during that time. They are listed below, and have been expanded upon further down. They are based on my experience from past relationships, observation of ladies I've known, my 18 years of marriage, and my knowledge of other people's marriages. Most of the points, I believe, are common sense. Of course, they are general guidelines only, so you'll need to see if they fit your own unique situation, and then choose what works for you:

1) Learn to recognise the signs
2) Take some pressure off your partner
3) Control your emotions
4) Don't inflame the situation
5) Don't attack or insult the person
6) If you do express anger, keep it short and about the subject
7) Understand that women feel better by venting their feelings
8) Understand that this is the time that women need to be loved the most

Learn to recognise the signs

One important piece of advice that I have personally found helpful is to learn to recognise when a woman is going through premenstrual so you can be understanding – as one prominent doctor once wrote in a book entitled "Man to Man about Women" by Dr James Dobson: *"Women certainly wish their husbands understood these physiological factors which play such an important role in the female body. Having never had a period it is difficult for a man to comprehend the bloated, sluggish feeling which motivates the wife's snappy remarks and irritability during the premenstrual period."*

One way of recognising when your partner is going through this difficult cycle is by taking careful note of her typical reactions. However, having done that, you may still find it difficult to know for sure if she has entered her cycle (sometimes she won't realise it either), but it's probably better to assume it to be the case anyway.

During this time, a woman often finds herself getting upset about things she would normally not worry so much about. I've personally found, a common sign that a woman has entered the menstrual cycle is when she suddenly starts getting upset about small things that her man does wrong or things that he doesn't do. She may also become a bit niggly or snappy – more than normal. This change of mood or behaviour seems to come out of the blue.

The advantage of recognizing when a woman is going through this time is that it gives you a better chance of responding in a more controlled way, instead of reacting negatively. And remember the overall principle: DONT TAKE IT PERSONALLY.

However, you need to know more detail about what to do, so hopefully the following common sense tips will help.

Take some pressure off her

One helpful thing you can do during this time is to try and take some pressure off her when you see your partner starting to stress out or get annoyed. For example, you may notice her getting irritable about things that are out of place. She may act as though the house was hit by a bombshell and comment that the whole place is a mess – but translated so men can understand, it probably really means: she is not feeling good, is finding it hard to cope, and needs a bit of help. So you need to do things such as: help with the kids, clean up the house and hang the cloths out etc. As for me, as soon as I sense my wife stressing out more than normal over things out of place etc, I have been known to immediately get to work with the vacuum and to engage my kids in a house tidy. It seems to help. Yes, I should do that more often at other times, but at least I know what to do – take the stress off her.

Control your emotions

One of the best things a man can do during this time of premenstrual tension is to simply stay in control of his emotions. In other words, don't overreact in a negative way. Of course it's a personal call, and it depends on individual circumstances, but, invariably, I personally have found it to be the best option and a good principle to keep in mind. Usually, it's not the time for tit for tat, justifying oneself, arguing the toss, or angry outbursts. It's more likely to be the time for keeping the peace, saying a simple sorry, or responding with other gentle answers. It may even be a time for expressions of affection, empathy and consolation – even if they're not well received. Now if you find my suggestions regarding giving affection and showing empathy, or being consoling during this time, a bit hard to comprehend or accept – you can read more about the topic further down in this chapter in the section entitled "It's the time they need to feel loved the most". It's quite a profound thing for a man to understand. Men, you can adopt one of two approaches during this time. You can either have a selfish approach, by taking the hump and thinking about how your own emotional needs are not being fulfilled – or you can choose to have a more loving outgoing approach, and start thinking about how you can supply your partners need for emotional stability. I strongly suggest the latter.

Having said the above, I realise that controlling your emotions is not always an easy thing to do. However, by reminding yourself that your wife is not feeling good because of strong hormonal influences – and that any negative remarks she makes are usually better not to be taken too personally, may help you to control your emotions. You might even find that you don't even have to grit your teeth or bite your tongue, though I'm sure none of you men ever do that. You're just too kind of course (hmm!).

Building emotional strength (control) is a bit like building up physical strength. It involves exercise, practise and happens over time. However, the rewards are positive, and if a man develops this kind of strength it promotes a more harmonious relationship with his partner. And by the way, controlling your emotions should not be thought of as weakness – the way some fake 'macho' men might think it to be. Rather, a woman is attracted to both physical strength and inner strength. And the ability to be strong emotionally is attractive to a woman. In contrast, a man who gets hurt too easily or who has a hair trigger temper, may in some women's minds, appear more like a big sook (Men, let them be the sooky bubs so you can cuddle them, but don't you become one yourself). This is not to say a man should cater to a woman's every whim or be under her thumb, and that subject is covered in a later chapter. Another thing that may help you to control your emotions during that time is to remember that following every premenstrual cycle is what I call a sweet cycle. It's when your wife will probably be feeling a little sexy and acting really sweet (provided you didn't mess up during the previous cycle of course). It's the time leading up to ovulation (her fertile time). Now you wouldn't want to miss out on loving her then, would you men? But be careful – unless you want more little bubs of course.

Don't inflame the situation

During a woman's premenstrual cycle is definitely not the time for men to bite back, lose their block, invalidate what women say, criticize them, make complaints, talk about marriage issues, walk out of the house in a huff, argue the toss, resort to name calling or anything else that would inflame the situation. One of the best analogies I can make to help guide the way you respond during this time is to suggest you think of it as a bit like playing cricket or baseball. If she bowls you a bouncer, up around your head, or throws you a curly one, somewhere below the belt, your best option is to swerve, duck and LET IT GO. Don't try and play it. In other words, keep as cool as a cucumber (control your emotions), and don't take it personally and get all hurt – and thus you'll avoid getting angry and inflaming what would normally not be such an issue. Molehills can be made into mountains during that time, so <u>depending on how a man reacts</u> and what he says, it's possible that sweet ladies could turn into raving maniacs (by the way, I got that expression from a lady that wrote a book about what men need to know about them). Men, if you don't believe what I'm saying, just ignore me and give it a test, but let me say, it's a hell of a way to learn, and I would hate to have to say I told you so. I would also hate to see you suffer as well as your partner. Men should especially avoid name calling, personal attacks, and insulting remarks. I will cover this subject in more detail.

Don't attack or insult the person

Whatever you do during your partner's premenstrual cycle never resort to name calling or attacking her as a person. Not only will she be shattered and emotionally destabilised if you do, but all hell will surely break loose. If you find yourself engaging in a dispute (not recommended) at least keep to the subject matter and don't attack the person. I'd also recommended that if you do express anger, to keep it short and about the subject. This subject will now be addressed in more detail.

Never, never insult your partner or call her a bitch or any other hurtful name, and especially don't swear

Many men in the heat of an argument with their partners (especially during their partners premenstrual time), make the fatal error of resorting to name calling or swearing. It's a grave mistake at any time, let alone during the premenstrual cycle. They refer to their partners using terms such as idiot, dumb, slut, and some men have even resorted to calling them a bitch. Now it's not my intention to give advice for every situation, and if you have done what I've described, I certainly don't know the personal details. However one thing I do know is that unless the relationship with your partner is already pretty much terminal, resorting to such tactics, instead of dealing with the issue in dispute, is not only shattering to her, but often deals an unforgettable blow to the relationship – which will affect it now and in the future. Unless your relationship resembles that of Bonnie and Clyde, doing that type of thing is simply divorce material, and should be avoided at all costs. Not only are harsh insulting words extremely difficult for a woman to forgive – she will never forget them. In fact, what usually happens is that what you said in past arguments will be brought up time and time again for years to come, as a part of new arguments. Thus, any future arguments will become more complicated and harder to resolve. If a man wants respect from a woman it needs to earned, but calling her names, swearing at her or putting her down is not the way it will come. Instead, she will just copy your behaviour and give back what you dish up to her. This should all be just common sense, but it is amazing how often men will react this way – especially during the premenstrual time.

Men, your partner is subject to strong hormonal influences during her cycle – she does not need to be yelled at, sworn at, called names, or to be subjected to any other form of verbal abuse. Rather she needs your love, patience and understanding.

What to do if a woman goes silent.

Sometimes during a woman's premenstrual cycle, depending on how you have reacted or what you have said, you might find your partner becoming angry, and as a result stops talking to you for a number of days. All women react differently of course, but some go quiet. You may actually regret how you have reacted or what you've said, and so I will now offer a little advice that has worked for me to redeem the situation. Below are some suggestions that might help:

1) Keep saying sorry, but don't expect instant results – it will take time for her mood to change.
2) Keep talking about things you need to communicate about, but don't worry if she doesn't respond for a few days.
3) Give her time to get over her mood.
4) Don't try to force her to talk
5) Relax – it will pass
6) Continue to do small acts of kindness for her, even though there's no reaction
7) Know that she will eventually feel better.
8) Sometimes a bunch of flowers or a gift will help her to gradually soften – but don't expect instant results.

Understand that women feel better when they vent their feelings

It's a well established fact expressed in many modern day books about marriage, that, unlike many men, a lot of women feel better if they talk or vent their feelings (subject is covered in the chapter entitled "Don't treat a cat like a dog"). It doesn't justify some of the things some women say or do, but at least it helps if you know that they actually feel better afterwards. In fact, you may often find that after taking something out on you, within about 5 minutes, women are often just fine, and act as though nothing has happened – provided you didn't snap back of course or try to invalidate what they said. (But, you don't do that. Do you men?...hmm!).

My general advice is: mostly let it ride, and try not to take any adverse things she might say too personally or too much to heart. And if you can avoid it – especially don't lapse into what I call a typical male silent sulk. In other words, snap out of it young man (or newly-wed), I know your feelings are hurt (I've been there), but it's really not as bad as you think. Besides, if you act like a blockhead a lot of the times, she probably will think that you have not got much feeling anyway. Just remember, she really loves you, but she just doesn't feel good at the moment. Why don't you wait a few days for her to feel good during her sweet cycle (fertile time)? It will be well worth it. Feel better now? I truly hope so, and may God be with you – he, he!

It's the time she needs your love the most

Something profound that most men don't seem to understand is, even though their women may appear to not want them around during the premenstrual period, it is during those times women actually need men's love the most. So please, don't suddenly run away, and don't go down the pub.

To draw an analogy, it's a bit like when your partner is sick. Is it really a good time to clear off and desert her, or is it better to stay and help her? If she was sick, I'm sure most men would stay and help. Yet, during the premenstrual time, some men purposely clear off, thus sending a strong message that they don't care – better translated "I don't love you". Yes, she may be moody, irritable and take things out on you, but you need to be understanding, and, as previously mentioned, not take it too personally. Rather than clear off, you should be thinking of how you can take some of the pressure off her. You should also continue to do all the little things mentioned in an earlier chapter that make a woman feel loved, even though it may appear that it is not appreciated at the time. Sure, it may appear as though she doesn't want you around, but the truth is it's the time she needs your love the most. It's the time she needs an unconditional type of love. In other words, the same love that people promise each other when they get married – to love each other in good times and bad. It's an opportunity to show her that you are always there – for better or for worse. In the long run it will convey the message that your love is genuine and sure, and be another reason why she will love you back. She will see you as strong, rock solid and it will build respect, which is always healthy in a man/woman relationship. Good luck.

SO YOU LOOK LIKE A GREAT DANE

Chapter 8

The kind of man a woman likes

This section is not meant to be discouraging, but to give you an idea of what women like in a man so you can subconsciously grow and develop over time. No, we don't have to strut around extending our necks like a Great Dane. We don't have to be perfect, but if you are truly interested in maintaining a good relationship with your partner it is helpful to at least be aware of the sort of things many women like. Some of the points are very basic, but you would be surprised at how ignorant some men appear to be. I therefore need to include them. And of course all women are individuals with their own likes and dislikes, but the following list is a good general guide, and worth thinking about.

A woman likes a man who is responsible

During years of running my filipinobrides.com.au website, one of the most common attributes women wrote on their profile forms was that they wanted a man who was responsible. In other words, they were not interested, for example, in some pot belly, idiot drunk who spends his time drinking with his mates to the neglect of his family. Nor were they attracted to men addicted to drugs or who gambled excessively. Men with holes in their pockets are simply not considered a good catch. Rather, they wanted someone that could take care of their family's physical and emotional needs. This is just common sense, but for the sake of some, it needs to be spelt out because unfortunately there are too many young men that get married, and carry on as though they were still single – when the truth is that women want someone who is responsible. They want someone who is responsible with finances, does his fair share of work in the house, and generally looks after the needs of the family.

A woman likes a man who is understanding

Another very common character trait that women wrote on their profile forms on my Filipino Brides website was that they wanted a man who is understanding. In other words, they like someone who could listen, understand their particular circumstances, how they felt, and then exhibit patience, empathy and compassion. They also, most importantly, wanted someone who understood a woman's needs – which is mainly what this whole book is about. This need for understanding is also the reason why some women I've talked to say they prefer older men. The reason is because, hopefully, through experience an older man has learnt to be more understanding. They also know that an older man is more likely to fall off the perch sooner, leaving all his money to them. Oops, did I say that! I'm joking.

A woman likes a man who is clean

It has been my personal observation over the years that women are generally cleaner than men. Yes, there are some very fussy men (and fuss pots), but I have noticed, even in the case of brothers and sisters that come from the same family, it is the females that seem to place more importance on cleanliness. Women seem to care more about detail in regards to cleanliness, whether it be the dishes, dust on shelves, dirt on your shirt, or hairs in the sink. Even their cars look spick and span. Whereas, some men's cars look more like rubbish dumps. Some women even go berserk if they see a few whiskers in the bathroom hand basin.

Now, I'm not saying that a man needs to be paranoid about the subject, but it definitely helps if he cares about his partner's desire to be clean and tries to accommodate where he can, within reason, as a matter of consideration and love.

A woman likes a man who smells nice

When I was young, my mum told me women like men who smell nice, and it's so true. So young men, please don't wait until your girlfriend or wife tells you that you PONG. It can be very embarrassing. Trust me on this one, because it happened to me when I was a dashing young bachelor, while I was trying to be impressive. Well, I sure was. The girl I was taking out was about as blunt as a meat axe. She just came straight out and said – POOH! I got the hint. It was a very bad way to learn, but I have never forgotten the lesson. Always remember, a bit of deodorant never goes astray. By the way, I once knew a girl who was turned on by a man who had been working all day, and had strong body odour. I believe sometimes that is true. I'm still trying to work that out, but to play safe I suggest you at least take into account my advice.

A woman likes a man who is loving.

This subject has been covered in an earlier chapter of this book entitled: "Women need to feel loved" – but, briefly, I am talking about what I call soft love. Some men call it mushy stuff. In other words, women need lots of cuddles and pats (not just when you want sex), and little acts of thoughtfulness and consideration – whether it be asking them if they would like a drink, buying them flowers or chocolates, opening the door for them, helping them with the dishes, cooking them breakfast, ringing them to say you're late, just listening to them without interruption, or other thoughtful little things you may do. All these little things send the same message – I love you.

This desire for a man who is loving was also commonly mentioned by ladies who registered on my Filipino Bride website. As mentioned, it's a soft type of love, and men need to learn what it is, even though there are times for a man to express a tougher variety (but good luck with doing that).

A woman likes a man who is confident

I have often heard a woman say she likes a man who is confident. By this, I mean a man who has healthy self esteem, and who is not easily affected negatively by a woman's criticisms – not someone who comes across as cocky or who puts on a Mr Macho act. Yes, we all have faults, and I'm sure some wives can be very quick to point them out – however, a man needs to put things into perspective. He needs to keep in mind that ALL have weaknesses, and that he is not unique. Rather than think negatively about himself, a man needs to focus on his strengths, learn to appreciate his abilities, and not be intimidated by any unkind remarks from the opposite sex. He also needs to keep in mind that men and woman are naturally weaker or stronger in different areas to each other, and by acknowledging this, not allow himself to suffer from unjustified low self esteem (as though he was of less worth than others) – when the fact is that we are all of value to others in different ways.

Yes, a man should take note of any of his wife's criticisms, but it does no good at all for the relationship if he starts thinking too negatively about himself because of any short comings he may have. It will just compound the situation. Rather, it's far healthier if he gets his mind off the SELF, and concentrates on the positive attributes he does have and applies them to his relationship. I have learnt to employ this principle over the years, and believe it has a more positive effect on relationships – compared to subjecting your partner to negative vibes about yourself. One of the reasons is because a woman will probably see this as a form of weakness, and not particularly like it. As the old saying goes: how can we expect others to love us if we can't even love ourselves?

A woman likes a man who has money and is generous

Well, if anybody takes exception to the above heading, just do a survey and ask women, who are looking for a marriage partner, whether they are more interested in a man who has a job. Or, better still, ask them if they think a lawyer would be a good catch or whether they like men with long pockets, as one lady I knew put it. Then do a comparison, and find out how many men would be interested in marrying a woman who is a lawyer, or how much it mattered if they married a woman who did not have a job. No, men and woman often look for different things, and one of the reasons women are different in this area is because they need to feel secure, and know that you will be able to provide the daily needs for them and their children. Yes, they like a man with money. No, you don't have to be rich, but probably the more you have the better they like it – don't you ladies? I reckon they probably like it about as much as men like sex. Some men and women even trade the two interests.

Woman love going shopping, and spending money – however, mostly on you, the children and things that are needed in the house (if you have not already noticed). They are natural homemakers. And yes, sure, they also like buying shoes, handbags, jewellery, makeup, and that kind of stuff. They will even buy you stuff if you are a good boy. No, not everybody is rich, and there are many happy marriages where the man is not, but there is no doubt that it helps the relationship if the man does his best to keep the money coming in, and that he is not overly tight with it. It has been my observation that Mr Scrooge is not the most popular man going around. However, if you are Mr Scrooge, don't despair too much because you just need to search harder for Mrs Scrooge, if you have not already found her. Remember, women do not usually marry men who they will have to provide for and support. Therefore, it stands to reason that unless you get sick, are too old to work or find yourself in unfortunate circumstances beyond your control it is probably not such a hot idea to give up your job and depend on your wife for support. If you do that, it's my belief that you may find it hard to maintain a woman's respect. This was the case with one lady, who once confided in me. She had a good job and found it difficult to respect her husband because he was only a handyman. In her case, she had a good job, and apparently earned more money than her husband. She may have had an attitude problem, but I'm sure her attitude is not unique.

Finally, before I leave this topic, there is one more thing I would like to say to young men, who are looking for a wife. Unless you go overseas and marry a Filipino or an Asian from a poorer country, it's probably not going to be your good looks that find you a wife. And it wouldn't matter if you looked like a Great

Dane or Elvis Presley, and made them laugh all the time. You need to be able to satisfy a woman's need for security. The difference is that Asians think white people have money, even if a white man does not have any or very much. Or, they at least think a white man has more than them. Usually, as soon a western woman finds out that a man has a low paid job or no job his chances of her wanting to marry him drops to zilch. Now you know why I am married to a Filipino. So my advice to a single man is to work hard at your career or occupation, save for the future, put a deposit on a house, and improve your chances dramatically of finding a partner.

A woman likes a man who stands up for himself with other men

One thing I have noticed over the years is that a woman admires a man who can stand up for himself with another man. Whether she observes that kind of thing at the movies or in real life situations it seems to go down well with her. I think the reason is because a woman sees it as strength and, generally speaking, women like strong men, whether it is physically, emotionally, psychologically or in character. No, there is no Mr Perfect, so it's no use stressing over this point, but I believe it to be a definite plus if a man develops the ability to stand up for himself with other men.

A woman likes a father who helps with the kids

One of the things that women consider when they are deciding on a marriage partner is whether men are good with kids, and would make good fathers. Not only good at playing with kids, but also good at keeping them under control. Sometimes kids can tend to run over their mothers (especially single mums), so it's important that a man supports his wife, and does not allow his children to be disrespectful to her. At these times, men need to exercise ability to be firm or strict – which includes using their deeper voice to good effect. So take charge men, use the volume in your voice, and try not to squeak.

A woman likes a man who is real

When I was a single young man, I remember someone telling me they heard a girl, that I liked, say that I was not real. At the time, I was quite baffled by this comment, and didn't really know what she meant. It was the first time I had really heard a comment like that from a female. Over time, I gradually got more of an idea of what women meant by the word 'real', when referring to members of the opposite sex.

Many years later, when I was in my early forties, another girl, who was interested in me, said she liked men that were real, and apparently she thought I fitted the bill. I believe the reason she saw me as a real person was because I was completely relaxed in her company and felt safe to be myself. In other words, being real to a woman means being the real you, and not trying too hard to make an impression and be someone you're not. Sometimes men try far too hard to be Mr Perfect or they become Mr Tippy Toe (especially if they are too hungry for sex from their wife). By doing this, they sometimes come across as a bit false and not really as themselves or as lacking confidence. So a good principle to keep in the back of your mind is: don't go <u>overboard</u> trying to please your wife's every whim, rather, be yourself , love yourself, and allow yourself to grow naturally over time. This topic is covered in more detail in a later chapter entitled: "Don't be Mr Plastic".

A woman likes a man who is in touch with his female side

Even though this book is about how men and women are different, as I have stated previously, it is not as though they are completely different. It's more a matter of being different in degree. Men do have a certain amount of female hormone that affects their behaviour, and some men have more than others.

According to one woman, who wrote on the internet, women are more attracted to men who are not afraid to show their feelings. I have also noticed this myself over time. For example, I had a man tell me once how women often complained that he never expressed any emotion. He was English, and apparently had a stereotypical, English, stiff upper lip disposition.

Women actually don't mind a bit of emotion, as long as it is of course not overboard (too female), and according to one lady: "they especially like it if it is obvious that you find them attractive, and there is nothing hotter than seeing how much we turn you on."

Regarding liking a sensitive man (some call it the new age sensitive man), what a woman means is that she likes a man to be caring and gentle with her feelings, and who is consoling. The reason a woman likes this is because her feelings are generally easier to hurt than a man's. Men need to be careful not to crush them.

A woman likes a man who is not too heavy.

By saying that a woman does not like a man who is too heavy, I'm not really talking about a man who is too fat, even though some women may say they don't like that either, and hen peck their husbands to lose weight. What I mean is that it has been my observation that a lot of women don't really like men who are overly strict, too intense, very serious or who talk too much to them about subjects like politics or religion – especially if they go on about that same subject for ages, and don't want to change subject. Take it from me. I've tried this on my wife and sisters. No, if you find the conversation is getting a little bit heavy for your partner, I suggest it's better to change the subject, and lighten up a bit. For example, have you ever noticed how many times a woman will change onto another subject when a man talks to her? This often frustrates men, but women seem to love it.

The concept of lightening up sometimes is supported by what women, who had registered on my Filipino website, said they were looking for in men. Many of them said they liked men with a sense of humour. This was also the case concerning a survey I saw on the internet about the same subject.

For some men, a sense of humour does not always come naturally, and not all women require this, but sometimes it may be better for a man to at least direct most of the heavy stuff toward other men, who would appreciate it, rather than just unloading it all on their female partner.

A woman likes a man who is strong emotionally.

A woman likes a man who can not only provide her with a shoulder to lean on, but a man who can also control his emotions. Concerning controlling emotions, a woman may not actually list this as a thing they like in a man, but it is definitely something a woman needs and likes, whether she realises it or not. In other words, a woman doesn't like a man who is too moody and easily offended. And they don't want a man who changes his mind all the time because of his emotions – who reacts to their every emotional reaction. Rather, what I believe a woman needs and likes is a man who can provide her with emotional stability and have a calming effect on her. In contrast to a man who just destabilises her emotional state of being. Yes, in other ways they like you to express emotion, but not really in the ways I have just listed. Good luck with doing that, but like building physical strength, you need to exercise your emotional restraint muscles, and over time become stronger. I've actually been aware of this for a long time, and have personally become stronger in this area over the years. It is good for the relationship.

A woman likes a man who is good with his hands

Women like a man who is good with his hands. In more ways than one I suppose, but what I'm talking about is a man who can do things around the house. While this is not a must have and many men today have not been taught those skills, it is always a plus. If you find that you are not so practical, you may need to employ tradesmen to take care of this area. The main thing is to fulfil your responsibility in regards to things that need to be done and fixed at your home. You can be sure that your wife will remind you.

More about the kind of man a woman likes

1) A man who has manners
2) A man who is thoughtful
3) A man who knows what he is doing
4) A man who is a bit hard to get
5) A man who helps around the house
6) A man who can make a decision
7) A man who is a good leader
8) A man who is physically strong
9) A man who protects them
10) A man who can plan ahead and set goals
11) A man who is a good provider
12) A man with long pockets
13) A man who owns a car
14) A man who is in a position of power
15) A man who is intelligent
16) A man with a sense of humour
17) A man who is affectionate

18) A man who owns his own house
19) A man who understands a woman
20) A man who is honest
21) A man who has a good job
22) A man who is kind
23) A man who is considerate
24) A man who smiles
25) Superman – joking

Men, don't get discouraged by all this, none of us are all these things. The main thing is to be yourself and love yourself. My advice is to just keep those things in the back of your mind, think on them from time to time, and allow your subconscious to have an effect. Also, gradually implement any adjustments in your behaviour that you feel comfortable in doing from time to time. But, don't push too hard and be Mr Plastic as I have explained in a later chapter.

ARE YOU A DOG OR A MOUSE?

Chapter 9

TSG

A woman does not respect a man who caters to her every whim

So far, we have discussed many things that a man can do to fulfil a woman's needs. However, I now want to balance the subject out a little by mentioning that a woman does not respect a man who caters to her every whim. In other words, a woman finds it difficult to respect a man who she can wrap around her little finger and who jumps to her every command. Yes, of course, I'm exaggerating the point, but I think it should be obvious that any self-respecting man should never compromise with what is right for the sake of appeasing emotional outbursts from his female partner.

Men, I'm not saying that it is always easy for you NOT to cater to a woman's whim. I believe the reason why it's not is because of the intense, intimate and emotionally charged nature of male/female relationships. And by taking such an approach your partner may temporarily not FEEL loved. However, in the longer term, I believe, it will probably produce the respect that every man needs in order to maintain a healthy relationship. It's been my experience that even though a woman may feel quite upset and angry, if a man stands his ground for what is right and just, she will really know when she is in the wrong, and given time, will see you as strong.

I believe the real issue, when you find yourself in such a situation, is 'how' you go about standing your ground, and whether the ground you are standing on is, in fact, firm. In other words, a man must firstly be sure he is doing the right thing. He then needs to control his emotions, be as diplomatic as possible, stick to the issue – and make sure he does not resort to name calling or insults. If you get angry, my general advice is keep it SHORT and direct it at the issue and not the person. A man should also try to avoid a spirit of bitterness and hatred. Furthermore, he needs to be careful about reacting back, if she reacts. Good luck with that one. What are you anyway, a dog or a mouse? – "a mouse" you say, oh, okay. Fair enough.

Be careful

Having said the above, a man needs to be careful not to fall into the trap of being contrary for the sake of pride or because he imagines himself to be in a power struggle or battle for control.

Men often express disagreement with their female partner in order to gain respect (which men crave). However, this will often achieve the opposite effect. Respect has a better chance to be gained if a man remains on firm ground and is resolute for the right reasons. Men, I know you want a woman to make you feel as though you are the top dog, but there are ways to achieve that feeling without resorting to always being contrary.

It's all about love and sex.

One of the main causes why some men tend to cater to a woman's every whim is because of their need for a woman's companionship, kisses, cuddles and SEX.

Yes men, I know you want the above, and I know what emotional blackmail is, and how some women can turn BIG MEN into panting, hungry puppy dogs or into a little mouse, but catering to a woman's every whim will not bring respect. Rather, my educated opinion is that men need to take a long term approach in order to have their needs fulfilled in that area, instead of focussing on "imagined" short term reward, and thus catering to whims (not needs).

Having now mentioned one cause of a man's tendency to cater to a woman's every whim, I would now like to convey some interesting information from an article I once read about what some women describe as "needy men". The following is a quote taken from a website on the internet and was written by a woman:

"Take it from a woman – guys who try too hard to impress a girl, end up putting her off. Do not look too needy or act desperate. Women have special sensory powers to sniff out men who try too hard. The last thing a woman wants is to have a clingy guy hanging outside her door. Be cool and confident, and trust me, she'll want you even more! Follow these basic rules and let your intuition guide you through the rest. Good luck!"

I have personally noticed the same thing that is written above. What really puts a woman off is the type of sex starved hungry look from men that is often spotted by women on a dance floor. They can see the guy coming for miles and take cover, usually by looking the other way or in other cases maybe heading for the toilet – and it doesn't seem to matter if the man looked like Elvis Presley. It's as though women had some sort of sensitive in build sex detecting radar system. If that's the case on the dance floor, why do we think a woman would feel any different about a man acting that way with whom she is in a relationship with – especially, when he starts to cater to her whims? So, as the lady above says, cool it a bit – and my advice is: keep the needy, desperate hot and steamy stuff for down the track until she's also reaches the point of sizzle. You can then mutually sizzle together, and there will be no problem.

DON'T BE FREAKY

Chapter 10

Don't be a control freak

In this section I give my personal view based on observation and experience. Take from it what you will. It's one thing to put your foot down, if your wife is doing something very immoral or wrong, and there is a time to do so – but it's quite another matter to dictate your wife's every move, and totally stifle her individualism for no good reason. In other words, act like a control freak or a little Hitler. Yes, I know this subject is not always straight forward, and some wives may be immature, spoilt, not able to handle money etc – and there are certainly times to say NO. I'm by no means an expert on every complex situation, however, in this chapter I would like to comment on three types of controlling attitudes I have observed over the years that have very negative consequences – and in many cases are best stopped and replaced with an opposite type of approach. The three types of controllers I would now like to write about are:

1) The insecure controller
2) The little Hitler
3) The controller who sees everything as a power struggle

The insecure controller

One of the reasons some men try to overly control their wives is because they feel insecure. In other words, they are plain scared of losing their partner, and afraid she will be attracted to another man. Now, it's quite natural to not want to lose someone who is so precious to you, but to have those feelings for no good reason – and then to let those emotions get out of control to the point that they start to destroy the relationship is a big problem. Now, I know there is probably more than one reason why some men are this way, but one common reason is because they have had a bad experience with an ex- girlfriend or wife in the past. To illustrate this point, I will now give a real example. The names of the individuals involved have been changed, but the story is true, and is as follows:

Bill fell madly in love with his girlfriend Mary, and wanted to marry her. When Bill met Mary, she had been going out with another man whose name was John.

However, John did not really show any significant romantic interest in her, but seemed to only want to be a friend – even though Mary was very interested in him. It was this time that Bill came along, and showed the interest in Mary that John never did.

Eventually, Mary decided to choose Bill as her partner, and they became boyfriend and girlfriend. They later moved in with each other, and lived together for six months. Bill was completely smitten and in love. However, unknown to Bill, Mary had never gotten John out of her system, and saw him from time to time at church. One day, when Bill was walking, he got the shock of his life because he saw John with his arm around Mary. Eventually, Mary left Bill to be with John. Bill was so devastated and hurt by what happened that he felt he could never trust another woman again.

After a number of years, Bill fell in love again with a lady he met called Helen. They went out with each other for two years. Up until that time, Bill and Helen had been enjoying a great relationship and did many things together. However, Helen had a lot of single girlfriends, and they began to invite her to go out to discos with them sometimes. For Helen, this was just a fun night out with her girl friends. They would all go there together, dance with each other, talk and have fun. It was just a typical girl's night out. However, for Bill, this became a bit too much, and he began to feel insecure, partly due to his experience with his former girlfriend Mary. And so, when he expressed his insecurity to Helen and said that he was not happy about the situation, she stopped going out with her friends. As a result, she inwardly felt stifled and upset – begrudging the fact that her friends were being taken away from her. And so, even though Bill had not ordered his girlfriend to stop going out with her friends, the fear of losing her had the effect of controlling her behaviour. In this case, his fear was not well founded because all she wanted to do was just spend some time with girlfriends.

Bill's insecurity was also compounded when Mary openly told him that her ex-boyfriend rang up at various times just to see how things were going. Even though she assured Bill that her ex-boyfriend was now only a friend, Bill still felt insecure. Eventually, Bill became so insecure that sometimes he would ring up just to see if Mary was still home. Another time, he tried to ring her one night, and found that her phone was busy. He then got so worried that she was having a long conversation with her ex-boyfriend that he then rang her ex-boyfriend, and asked if he had been talking to her. The ex-boyfriend said no, and suggested to John not to hold on too tight to the relationship because he would just end up losing her. In this particular case, Bill's fear was really unjustified because the relationship between him and Helen had been quite strong. However, since John had began to feel insecure and allowed his emotions to get out of control, he had put unnecessary pressure on the relationship – and eventually Helen felt so stifled that the relationship suddenly just SPLIT.

The above is an example of what I call the insecure controller. In other words, even though Bill did not directly order Helen to stop talking to her ex-boyfriend or stop going out with her girlfriends, he did show her his unhappiness and FEAR – which made her feel stifled and gave her the feeling that he was always looking over her shoulder. The moral of the story is that you probably have more chance of keeping your relationship with your wife or partner by letting go a bit (especially if she has done nothing wrong and the relationship is strong) – than if you try and hold on too tight. And so, it's better not to allow past experiences with a different women to affect your relationship with someone else for no valid reason. If a woman has done nothing to destroy your trust, then don't allow fear to destroy something that is not broke (the relationship).

In another situation, which I knew about, a man was so fearful his wife was going to leave him for another man that he did not only forbid her from getting a job, but got worried if she so much as spoke to another man at the shop. The reason he acted in this manner was because of his former wife's behaviour, and not because of the behaviour of his present wife. He chose to deal with his emotions by getting get drunk. In his case, it was a form of control by acting in a certain way – getting drunk.

In other cases, a man's insecurity can escalate to the point of getting very jealous, where malice or hatred may become involved. When that happens, there may be a tendency for some men to want to punch someone's lights out for looking sideways at their wife or partner. In other cases the jealous man may make threats or use violence against his wife in order to control her behaviour – even though her behaviour may be innocent. In some situations, this happens because the relationship is on the rocks, and the husband's insecurity is well founded. However, instead of trying to address the causes for the problems, the man attempts to keep the relationship together by making threats or performing acts of violence. And so the cycle continues. That approach simply will not work. The only hope of "controlling" a wife is to love her, and if that doesn't work nothing else will.

It's been my observation that if a relationship is good and loving it is unusual for a women to be unfaithful. One exception to that would be if a woman married a man for the wrong reasons (maybe for money), and did not really love him.

The little Hitler

The other type of controller is what I call the little Hitler. The little Hitler type of controller, that I will be describing in this section, is a dictator – a man that does not include his wife in the decision making process, and wants to impose such things on his wife as his own religion, personal likes and dislikes etc. Basically, he wants to control everything including how the house is furnished, what food she buys and eats, the way she decorates the house, what clothes she buys and how she spends every last cent. I became very familiar with one such relationship, which I will now give some detail about.

I have changed the names to protect their identity. The names I have given them are Ben and Sue. When I first met Ben he was very interested in meeting an Asian lady, probably because he was looking for someone who would be submissive. When I interviewed him, I became aware that he was very religious, and had strong ideas about the man being the head of the family. I noticed he was very opinionated in his ideas, and was a very strict vegetarian. He was also very extreme with money, and apparently could sustain his life on the smell of an oily rag, so to speak. He was also a perfectionist. Eventually, he took a trip overseas to meet some ladies he had been writing to. Little did I know at that stage, one of the reasons he was interested in an

Asian lady was probably because he had the idea they were very subservient.

As it turned out, he evidently wanted someone to wait on him hand and foot – a woman who would bow and scrape to his every whim. It seemed that he was preoccupied with what a wife could do for him rather than what he could do for her, which is a very self centred approach indeed. Eventually he found a young Asian lady who seemed to fit the bill. Apparently, during courtship, she was so keen that she catered to his every desire. One of the reasons she was interested in him was because she liked the fact that he was religious. She eventually agreed to marry him. At the wedding reception his self centred attitude seemed to express itself, when wedding guests were left hungry. When he got married, his approach was total dictatorship. He imposed his religious beliefs on his wife, restricted her food to vegetarian, was paranoid about her putting on weight, and basically tried to have control over her to the point that she could not express her individuality and her many likes and dislikes. He also went to the extreme of trying to control her behaviour by punishing her for what he considered bad behaviour. As a result, the relationship became very rocky, and he then resorted to trying to control the situation by assaulting her physically. Eventually, the relationship ended in divorce.

Now this, of course, is an extreme example of what I call a dictator or little Hitler type of controller, but it does serve to illustrate a point. The point being: a man needs to allow his wife or partner to express her individuality, and not stifle her by trying to control her every move, desire and action. Some men seem to have a dream of having a subservient wife that waits on them hand and foot, and that complies with their every command.

Well, okay, maybe all men. However, this is simply a dream, and has little to do with reality. The truth is that women have individual minds, and should be free to express their opinions, likes, dislikes and ways of doing things. Women see things differently than men, and this should always be taken into consideration and accommodated.

Another man I knew tried to control his wife to the point that he basically gave her no money, and so she had to ask him every time she wanted to buy something. She was not allowed even to buy a plant for the house without asking for his permission – and if he didn't like it, the answer was no. He also dictated what clothes she could buy for herself, and as far as lady like items, he just thought it was a waste of money, and stopped her from buying them. In these sorts of relationships the woman loses her personal identity, feels stifled and smothered. It becomes a totally selfish and unloving approach, and her emotional need to express her individuality is totally crushed. Inevitably, that couple ended up in a bitter divorce, in which the man involved tried to take full custody of his children in a desperate attempt to have full power over them. The above, Hitler type approach is a recipe for disaster. Oppressive dictators over nations are eventually overthrown, and the same is true of these sorts of husbands. As one man said on a radio program I once heard, "women need their own space". He said: *"he and his wife were very different, and that the key to success in their marriage was that they gave each other SPACE to be themselves"* It should never be a one way street just because you are the man. It's also been my observation that women need to feel they are part of a team, and should be included in the decision making process in some way. In other words, they need to <u>feel</u> that you care about their needs and desires, as well as your own. The only sort of power and control a husband should seek to have over his wife is the power and control that comes through loving her in the ways that have been detailed in this book so far. It is far more likely to result in a wife who wants to please you and fulfil some of your desires and needs. Think of her needs first, and you may find that she returns that love to you. If you want her to follow you, just set a good example, and let her follow that.

The controller who sees everything as a power struggle

The third type of controller that I will now address is a man who seems to feel that almost every interaction with his wife is some sort of struggle for power – whether that interaction with her includes her advice, criticism, disagreement on a topic, or her attempts to help and fill a void.

There are at least three possible reasons why I think some men feel this way, which I will now address.

4) Low self esteem
5) Pride
6) Feelings of disrespect

Low self esteem

Low self-esteem can be a problem with both men and women. However, in my opinion, in the case of a man, it can reflect itself by him trying to assert ascendancy over a woman, when she offers her opinion or advice. Consequently, instead of appreciating what may be good advice or understand that she is just trying to help him, it has the effect of making him feel small or inferior, and is therefore instantaneously rejected. Sometimes the reason for this is because the man may have had an overbearing mother, and therefore feels his wife or partner is treating him the same way – as though he were a little boy, and not a grown up man.

A man generally doesn't like to be bossed around by a woman, and sometimes he feels that this is the case. Sometimes when a woman tries to help her husband, offer advice, or corrects him it is perceived as a threat to the relationship. He feels he is being bossed around, and if he allows his partner to do that she will lose respected for him. Fearing that, he struggles to gain control over her. This approach is a big mistake, and just causes unnecessary trouble. Men need to understand that it is a natural inclination for a woman to try and help him, and it's not usually about power or control. In fact, in general, a woman is not competitive by nature, compared to a man.

Feelings of disrespect

It has been my experience, that because small things matter to women more than men, there is a tendency for a woman to be what some men call 'picky'. Sometimes the result is that the man feels disrespected. Once again, he knows that, if it was true, it would be bad for the relationship. So in an attempt to gain respect, he enters into a kind of power struggle by rejecting everything she says or by putting her down.

Pride

Sometimes feelings of superiority can have the same effect as inferiority or low self-esteem. This seems to be the case when a man is academically more advanced than his woman partner, and assumes he always knows best. Consequently, he is quick to dismiss her ideas or to put her down. In his puffed up view of himself, he rejects what may have been a good idea – lest his elevated opinion of himself be humbled somewhat. In other cases, men simply want a woman to look up to them, and that desired posture seems threatened if a woman is constantly disagreeing or correcting him.

That concludes my experience regarding different types of controlling men. The approaches mentioned in this chapter have negative effects on relationships between a man and a woman. At the very least, men need to be aware of these type of controlling attitudes, and do their best to avoid them, if they can.

DON'T BE MR PLASTIC

Chapter 11

JWG

Don't try too hard to be what you are not

Having now gained a bit of an idea about some basic principles mentioned in previous chapters, there is another principle I would like to explain, which, hopefully, will help prevent some men from going overboard with their new found knowledge – and that is: "Women do not like plastic men". In other words, a man who pretends or tries too hard to be what he is not. It turns women off. The bottom line is that we are what we are, and knowledge about how to treat a woman can only be digested and assimilated into our inner being gradually over a lifetime, until it becomes more of what we are. Putting it another way, it's not a good idea for a man to rush out tomorrow and try to be an instant

Mr Perfect because all he will do is become an instant Mr Plastic. Women are people, people. From my experience and from reading about the subject, a woman is good at observing body language, picking up small inflections in a man's voice, and will soon recognize if a man is not being a real person.

So please men, don't rush out tomorrow, like a chook with its head cut off, and try suddenly to be a different man. Just be a different man, in the sense that your attitude has changed, as a result of having gained more knowledge about male/female relationships, and because of a decision to embark on a lifelong learning and implementation of such knowledge.

Women like men who are real

Women like a man who is a real person. To illustrate what I mean, I will now give you a true life example. I have changed the names in the following account, but the story is fairly accurate.

Over the years Jack had heard women refer to some men as NOT real people, and didn't take much notice. The inference being that they preferred men who were real. Anyway, time went by and Jack was in his thirties. During that period he was attending a camp for single men and women. At the camp there was a girl named Jill, who he really liked. In fact, he was emotionally involved with her. She was not his girlfriend, but he went out with her as a friend occasionally. It was during the time at the camp, that a person called Tom overheard Jill say that Jack was not a real person. Tom then told Jack what Jill had said. When Jack first heard what Jill had said about him, he didn't really didn't know what to make of it and whether it was good or bad.

It was a bit like another occasion when someone told him they had heard a lady say that he brought out her mother instincts. He didn't know if she meant that he was like a little sooky bubba or that she was so attracted to him that she just wanted to cuddle him. He was confused. He was confused then, and he was now confused again, having been told how Jill had said he was not a real person. He probably would have preferred if she had referred to him as unreal, which would have sounded more like a compliment.

Anyway, time passed by. Meantime, Jack kept that incident in his mind, and gradually began to work out what a woman means when she refers to a man as not real. The subject finally became very clear when he met another lady named Joan, who was very interested in him. However, unfortunately, Jack was not really interested in her, other than being a friend. Joan said that one of the reasons she really liked Jack was because he was a REAL person. But WHY – why did she think he was real and what did she mean? And why was he referred to by Joan as real, and by Jill as not real? Well, the reason was because Jack was not really interested or emotionally involved with Joan romantically, and as a result, was completely relaxed and himself. He joked and laughed with her, and she was able to connect with his true feelings, which women like. In other words, he was NOT trying to impress or be someone he was not, and so what she saw was the real him. It was then, Jack began to realise what Jill had meant when she said he was not real. At that time, Jack was emotionally involved with Jill and was trying too hard to impress – so his real feelings did not come out. Instead, he came across as a plastic person or not real.

Consequently, I guess you could say that just like the old nursery rhyme about when 'Jack and Jill went up the hill', things did not work out too well.

This example, also explains why, in my own younger days, most of the girls that were attracted to me were the ones I was not really attracted to. It was because in their company I was being myself and felt completely relaxed. Whereas, in the company of girls who I was really attracted to or emotionally involved with, I found myself freezing up or trying too hard to impress. As a result, the real me and how I truly felt about things did not come out. It seemed that as soon as I became overly attracted to a girl, I really liked, the chances of her being attracted to me was pretty much zilch.

So why am I saying all this. Well, the reason is because I believe the same applies to your wife or female partner. They will love you more if you are yourself, so don't try too hard to be what you are NOT. In other words, don't be Mr Plastic.

MORE STUFF TO KEEP YOU OUT OF THE DOGHOUSE

Chapter 12

Other helpful tips for men

The Doghouse is a very cold, lonely place, and unfortunately some men spend too much time there. In this chapter are a number of tips to help keep you out. Once again, I have taken into account what I consider are some of the general differences between men and women – so chances are they may well fit your individual situation.

Women need to feel connected

I thought I would put this topic at the beginning of this chapter. The reason for this is because feeling connected, according to one book I read, is one of the most important needs that a woman has – yet the concept is one of the least understood by men. I must confess that I did not have much of an idea myself what women mean by the term 'connect' until recently. In fact, I'm still coming to grips with the subject, but it's too important a subject for a man to understand to leave out of this book. I hope to at least give you some idea about what a woman means by the term, and leave the rest for you to work out yourselves.

Ladies, I know this is such a simple subject for you, as other subjects in this book, and you may be wondering why men have difficulty with it, but let me suggest that it may have something to do with the fact that you are a woman and not a man. However, what this subject does illustrate, once again, is that there are basic differences between a man and a woman, and how hard it can be for them to relate to one another at times.

Having stated the above, I will now attempt to help my fellow man understand what a woman means when she expresses her desire to connect with her male partner. Generally speaking, women are better at forming intimate relationships with other woman in contrast to men doing the same with other men. Unlike women, men don't hold hands, put their arms around one another, dance with each other as much or call each other darling. It's another example of the difference between the sexes. Usually a man's relationship with another man is not as intimate as a woman's relationship with another woman. The reason for this is because a woman is more interested in relationships than a man, involving intimate sharing of feelings and problems. They even go to the toilet together just so they can talk.

In contrast, men are often quite content to share experiences like working together, and in that way form a bond with other men. And they especially aren't interested in going to the toilet to talk with each other. They are quite content to talk about THINGS (like football or cricket) as opposed to talking about relationships, and how they FEEL. They are also not so inclined to talk about their problems or relationships, whereas, women like to go further than talking about things. They also like to share their feelings with one another.

Consequently, regarding a woman's relationship with her male partner, even though they may have spent a lot of time together, if the man has just talked about THINGS and not shared his FEELINGS, the woman may feel disconnected. A woman likes to have an intimate relationship with her man, which involves mutual sharing of feelings about things with each other. You may notice that there is a subtle difference between sharing feelings about things, in contrast to just talking about things. Sharing your feelings is more about you as a person and what makes you tick. It makes a woman feel closer and more connected. It also makes women feel secure in the relationship. For example, if a woman notices that you have something on your mind, but you keep it to yourself, she may start imagining that there is a problem in the relationship, and start thinking that you are unhappy with her or don't love her.

A man sharing his feelings is also the main attraction for a woman making love with a man – they like the intimacy involved in vocalising and sharing feelings (if a man is accommodating). In contrast, men have a tendency to keep feelings to themselves.

Now that you have, at least, some idea of what women mean by the word 'connection' and that it is a basic need for a woman to feel this way, what can a man do to accommodate this need? Well, I suppose you could try having sex more often, I guess, but I'm not sure of your chances. My suggestion is to at least be aware of a woman's need to feel connected, and let it penetrate your subconscious by thinking about the subject from time to time. Then, as you sense a woman's need, gradually get better at accommodating her need as part of an overall attitude of maintaining and improving your relationship. Remember, Rome was not built in a day. However we can endeavour to gradually develop in that area. Women call it getting in touch with your feelings. But men, can you please do it without changing into a woman. They don't like that either. In other words, don't overdo it, and especially don't cry too much. Good luck with that.

Sometimes a woman would like you to read her mind

Sometimes, a woman will not come straight out and ask for something. Instead, they will hint. For example, you may be at a party or dance and forget to ask them if they would like a drink. As a result, sometimes they will throw some sort of hint your way, and hope you are at least sensitive enough to realise what they need and subsequently provide it for them. However, a woman will probably feel more loved if she didn't have to hint, and that you had thought of her needs or desires all by yourself. Generally, they like a man who is thoughtful, and who thinks about their needs without having to be asked. Also, sometimes when a woman goes quiet, and you ask her what's wrong, she sometimes doesn't really want to have to tell you. They may say that nothing is wrong, but in an unconvincing way, indicating that there is something wrong. Often this takes place when a woman feels you have wronged her in some way, and she wants YOU to think of what you have done to upset her, rather than have to spell things out to you. One real life example of this was when a certain man's wife went silent because he forgot her birthday. She said nothing to remind him. I suspect she wanted to see if he would remember later during the day, all by himself, and then see his reaction. Luckily, he did remember about midday and turned the dinner outing, which they were attending, into her birthday celebration. He also expressed remorse, and did other things later in the day to make up for his bad memory. It seemed to work.

Don't treat a woman like an object

Most men have probably heard at some time in their lives that women don't like being treated like objects, but how many men have really stopped to understand what they mean? It's important to understand this because it is such a basic subject, and if you don't know what they mean, frankly, you may find that having sex with your wife (if she still lets you) will be like having sex with a dead fish or a blow up doll. The reason for this is because you have probably made her feel that way – like an object or non living creature. The reason women are sometimes made to feel this way is because of what I call a blockhead mentality towards sex by some men. In other words, it's a self indulgent, beast or Rottweiler type of sex – which usually only lasts about two minutes and lacks love and feeling. Yes, the guy has a whale of a time, but not her. It's more like rape, some may say. So keep in mind that a woman does not like to be treated like an object, and it is a reason why some women no longer want to have sex with their partner.

Rather than do this, a husband needs to read the chapter in this book entitled "Rottweiler Guide to Love and Sex " and also the chapter about what makes a woman feel loved. They also need to learn to hug their wives more often during the day, rather than just when they want sex. Woman like it when men give them lots of cuddles. It shows them that you really love them, rather than a woman thinking you just do it to get sex.

,

Need to spend time with your partner

Over the years, I have noticed that one cause of many divorces is when the husband works away for regular extended periods of time. Whether he drives a truck interstate, works at mines, frequently travels overseas or interstate for business, time away often puts pressure on the relationship. I'm certainly not saying that all marriages, where this is the case, are doomed to failure, and I realise that people do not always have the luxury of being able to choose their circumstances. Also, people's financial situations certainly can't always be ignored. However, if you do find yourself in this situation, you need to consider if the situation is putting strain on your relationship – and whether there is anything you can do to change things without causing other problems that would also have a negative effect. I realise that, sometimes, it can be a catch twenty two situation, and you may need to decide what is the lesser of two evils. Having stated the above, there may be several reasons why spending regular long periods of time away from your wife/partner may not be such a crash hot idea (even though you get more money). They are as follows:

1) She may find it difficult to cope with the loneliness
2) You may drift too far apart
3) Women like to feel close and intimately connected, but can't really feel this way when you are away most of the time
4) By being away it may be harder to make them FEEL loved – they may also think that you value money more than them.
5) Women just like time together with the one they love.

Apart from working away for regular and extended periods of time, one definite no-no for married men is to continue to act like single men by spending too much time drinking with their mates down the pub or doing things like going fishing all the time. Now, I'm not saying that husbands and wives should not give each other personal space, but if it reaches the point that your wife feels a big second in your life and that you don't love her, you then need to think about your priorities. The reason for this is because one day your wife may just walk out and no longer be there. Especially, if you always come home intoxicated, start acting like a typical blockhead, vomit like a dog all over the floor, and then wonder what's wrong with HER.

Woman need to feel needed

During the course of my life, I have observed some ladies that have become disenchanted at times because they felt as though their male husband or partner did not really need or want her help. It's been my understanding for years that ladies have a strong desire to help their partner, and need to feel needed. In saying that, I mean needed by someone they love.

Having said the above, I believe there are many reasons a woman may feel not needed, when they actually need to be needed. For example, it may be because their male partner is very capable at pretty much everything, including cooking, cleaning, vacuuming, washing, ironing and even dusting. He may even be good at cutting his nails or applying lipstick if men were to wear such stuff. Now, don't get me wrong, a woman really appreciates a man who helps around the house, and there may be some women who are reading this right now who can't see a problem and want me to shut up! However, if a man does those things to such an extent that he makes a woman feel a bit useless, with nothing to do, you may find she feels not needed, when she needs to feel needed. Clear as mud. Good.

In other cases, a woman is sometimes made to feel not needed when her partner is doing work fixing the house. For example, she may try to help him, but the man perceives her as being bossy and puts her down. Other times he may just undiplomatically reject her help because he feels she will just slow him down. In these cases, it may pay a man to consider that maybe she is, in fact just trying to help him, and he needs to be very diplomatic and caring.

Now there may be other reasons a woman may feel not needed, and so, if you find that to be the case with your partner, here are a few tips that may help solve the problem:

1) Compliment her when she cooks a really tasty meal.
2) If you're working on a house project, let her help a bit, even if it does slow you down.
3) Generally show appreciation for the work she does.
4) Don't do everything in the house yourself, and ask her to help.

Having said the above, I think the problem of men doing too much work around the house is not so common, and if they do, chances are they don't do as good a job – especially with the dusting. So, as long as your female partner doesn't feel like they are your mother, you are probably on safe ground.

Women don't want to be your mother

Having said the above, it's important also to state that women don't want the opposite either. In other words, they don't want to be your mother. Rather, they want someone who shares in the day to day responsibility of life: the home, chores, looking after kids, finances, and everything else. A woman wants a man who will do what is needed without having to be told, make decisions, and they want to be with someone they do not have to nag. They did not get married to care for a grown adult who acts like a child, but to have a partner who will share in responsibilities. One of the biggest problems I think many men have is laziness. Or is it just me, hmm!

Late is a four letter word

Imagine the following scenario. It's Friday and Joe Blo knocks off work and decides to go down the pub for a few drinks after a hard day. Meanwhile, his wife Sue is busy in the kitchen making Joe Blo his favourite meal. She has even gone to the trouble of preparing a special desert. In anticipation of his arrival, she keeps the food on low heat and waits. In the meantime, down the pub, one drink leads to another and Joe Blo gets half done, and forgets all about the time. Before long, Joe realises the time has passed 9pm. He then decides to bolt for the door, stumbles, gets up and makes his way home. In the meantime, the food on the stove has gone dry and been turned off. It now sits cold on the stove. But not Sue – she is steaming hot. You see, it was not the first time Joe Blo had been late. Well, you may be able to guess the rest of the story, but in short Joe Blo ends up with the food in his face, instead of in his mouth. Being late like Joe is bad news – don't be! Especially, if you know you will be late, and don't even ring her. Whether you are running late from work or whatever the situation, you need to ring her. Not to do so is to send her a message that you don't love her. In the case of Joe Blo, it was a double whammy because not only did he not ring, but he showed that he cared about his mates more than her. In relationships, late is a four letter word.

A woman will learn your ways

One attribute that seems to be a particular trait of women is their tendency to copy the behaviour of their man, whether it is good behaviour or BAD. Copying other people's behaviour is of course not uncommon among males and females, but I have particularly noticed this sort of thing among women who are in bad marriages. In one case that I was familiar with, a husband complained about the way his wife treated him. The funny thing about it was that he did not realise that his wife was apparently getting her own back, having learnt from HIM. It's called sweet revenge. He complained his wife embarrassed him greatly, by criticizing him in front of his business client. I later learnt from another woman, who knew about their relationship, that the reason she did that was because her husband had previously done the same sort of thing to her, by putting her down in front of others.

In another example, a man in a bad marriage, which ended up in divorce, said that his wife constantly complained. It was rather funny that he should say that, because I have rarely seen a greater complainer than him. At the time, it made me wonder if she had learnt it from him. The moral of the story is, if we find our wife or partner is doing negative things towards us, it might be a good idea to check whether we taught them what to do. It's certainly worthwhile checking. Apart from those examples, I have noticed in a number of marriages between Filipino ladies and Australian men, where the lady had, apparently, picked up the habit of using the F word during the course of the marriage. I can only think they probably picked up the habit from their husbands, who I know swore in front of them or at them. The reason I say this is because swearing by Filipino ladies, who came from the provinces in the past, appears to be not so common – especially using the F word. Their Catholic upbringing may also have had an influence. At any rate, I believe it is fairly safe to say that if a man swears at his wife he is teaching her what to do, and she will probably do the same thing back at him. You then need to ask yourself whether you really want that – considering that, I believe, they are very good at copying your behaviour.

Women need someone who is always there

During the course of my lifetime, I have come to perceive how a woman needs a man who is always there, and what that means. I have come to understand that a woman needs a man to be there in the following ways:

1) Your physical presence
2) Your love
3) Your support and encouragement
4) Your emotional stability
5) Your commitment

Your physical presence

This subject has already been partially covered in the section under the heading 'need to spend time with your partner'. If a man spends too much time working, fishing and going to the pub with the boys it often translates to a woman that you don't love her.

Your love

As discussed in an earlier chapter, a man needs to make his partner/wife feel loved. He needs to show that love is still there despite the turbulence, hurdles and bumps that the relationship may experience. It's not always easy, but sometimes men need to take a deep breath, get over conflicts or annoyance, and continue to provide an unconditional type of love.

Your support and encouragement

You need to be there for your woman in the good times and the bad times. Whether it is in times of severe bereavement or when she is going through other kinds of emotional stress or anxiety – you need to be there for her by just letting her express her feelings, and not interrupting or offering unwanted solutions (already discussed in another chapter). She may also, during those times, need your hugs. You also need to be there in the fun times – whether it is accompanying her when she is invited to go to a party by her friends or attending events that she is interested in. Yes, there are times when you may not always choose to go, but it's worth putting in some effort if you feel it would be good for the relationship. I remember my wife saying how she appreciated me always being there for her by going with her to many parties so she could enjoy social occasions with her work friends.

Your emotional stability

Losing control of your emotions in fits of anger, putting your partner down and name calling makes a woman feel insecure in the relationship and think that you may not always be there. Some men also let emotions get out of control, and threaten to leave. They do it hoping to solve problems in the relationship, through force or blackmail. However, all this does is put the relationship more at risk and creates instability and insecurity. It's a big mistake that I learnt not to do years ago. I remember a number of men, who were married to Filipino ladies, make the fatal mistake of threatening to send their wives back to the Philippines in the first year or so of marriage. Their marriages ended in divorce. Now it's not for me to know the circumstances of their marriage relationships, but one thing I was consciously careful NEVER to do myself was to make such a threat to my wife, no matter what trying issues came up between us. The reason I made sure I did not do that was because I understood that a woman preferred a man who she could rely upon to always be there. A man whose love and commitment she could depend on. The other thing I have been extremely careful not to do is NEVER to put my wife down or verbally abuse her by calling her names. To me, its dynamite and something that women never forget because of their hurt feelings. In fact, if men do that, the topic will come up again years later and complicate other arguments. Rather, the best thing a man can do is control his emotions, and give his partner/wife the feeling that he is always there.

Your commitment

If you are married, you made a commitment to love and stay with your wife. For a woman's emotional stability, I believe she needs to feel commitment. Men can give that feeling by having an attitude of commitment – even when things get tough. The commitment should be, to always work through or around the problems and never give up. Yes, there may be times when you may not feel like it, but my advice is to take a deep breath, have a break to think about nothing for a while (often called opening the nothing box in our brain), have a coffee or beer (but not too much), and carry on later. By the way, ladies may not understand my advice to you men because apparently they don't have what is called a nothing box in their brain.

THE 20 COMMANDMENTS FOR PIT BULLS

Chapter 13

For men only

Ladies, what on earth are you doing here? I'm shocked. Didn't you see the 'Men Only' sign on the door'? Don't you know that being here is like coming to a buck show full of Pit bulls and blockheads? Okay then, I guess I'm not really surprised that you are reading this chapter. I just hope some men are reading it too. In fact, I hope my book is not only read by women, who really bought it for their husbands.

Anyway, here is where some may call me a chauvinist pig – but in this chapter I need to talk like a man to your man, and I can't afford to beat around the bush. I only hope you have read the previous chapters, and not gone straight to this one. It's just a risk I have to take because there are far too many men TREATING WOMEN LIKE MEN, and in so doing they trample all over their feelings – not realising how clumsy or heavy they are and how much it hurts. Men, I will make this chapter short and sweet. It's a little tongue in cheek and over the top, but remember, "many a true word is spoken in jest" – and my intention is to simply exaggerate the mental differences between a man and a woman. The reason for this is so your expectations are realistic, and you can learn to accept a woman as she is, and love her in the true sense of the word. I hope it helps. See below, a simplistic set of rules for men ONLY – break them at your own peril. Ladies please don't read the rules, but I know you will for sure. So when you do, please remember that the rules were made to help your Goodman, Beginner or Blockhead to give you the love that every woman needs:

1) Thou, oh man, shalt wipe thy dirty boots before thou enter thine house.

2) Thou shalt NOT be the one to teach thy wife to drive thy car – lest thy marriage end in divorce.

3) Thy wife is in charge of thy kitchen and house – not thou. Anyway, I've seen too many messy bachelor pads. Don't knock it.

4) Thou shalt by all means allow thy wife to hit thee, but thou shalt NEVER hit thy wife – anyway, if she does, it's really a

compliment because she thinks you are strong and can't feel it. Only, remember not to let her see you cry.

5) Thou art forbidden to nag thy wife lest she thinkest thou art acting like a woman.

6) Thou shalt learn to say YES to thy beloved wife lest thou be deprived of thy favourite lust.

7) Wives canst lose thy temper with thy husband, but husbands thou DON'T.

8) Thou shalt tell thy wife sweet little lies about her appearance or meals she serves you. Besides I heard that in a song with the lyrics "tell me lies, tell me sweet little lies"

9) It is a woman's prerogative to change herst mind seven times a day, but thou oh man art forbidden.

10) Oh thou man, be understanding if thine woman gets hurt for small things, but thou 'oh man', be hard like rock or pretend.

11) Oh man, feelest not discouraged if thou feel dameth if thou do or dameth if thou don't. The reason for this is because thou art dameth if thou do or dameth if thou don't. Thou shalt accept this situation. It is normality.

12) When thy wife gets hurt or goes silent thou shalt be compassionate and patient. However, forbid this with thyself, lest thou appear a big sook.

13) Look mercifully upon thy wife, when she knowest not what to do – but, why oh man dost thou not knoweth?

14) Woman, feelest free to taketh thou a wrong turn and get lost in thy car, but thou man DON'T – lest you suffer great WRATH (before the day of judgement from the Lord actually happens).

15) Give thy wife plenty of money.

16) If thy woman mentions that she needs to connect, do not thinketh she is talking about sex.

17) Thou shalt never tell thy wife she is fat, even if she is fat.

18) If thy wife asks what thou art thinking? Do not say nothing, even if the answer is nothing.

19) SAY SORRY – often.

20) Generally, shut up and do what you're told.

Men, don't try and reason around these rules or say they are not fair, and that I'm hard on you because I already know I'm being hard. Just obey the twenty commandments, because you will find that things will work better. If you are not good at doing these things don't worry too much, and give yourself time to gradually develop in these areas. It's like when a man exercises physically; he becomes stronger. This chapter is mostly about controlling your emotions so you don't hurt your partner's feelings. Instead of doing that, a man needs to be loving and understanding and give a woman the emotional stability she needs.

BORING STUFF

Chapter 14

It's about plain hard work

Sorry men for making this chapter boring and I don't think you will really like it, but I just could not leave this subject out of the book. Today, many married men fail to really appreciate the work load that their wives are under. And, unfortunately, many don't do their reasonable share of work in the house. I include myself. Mothers with small children have to cope with extremely long working hours that stretch into the night, seven days a week. The same applies to working mothers, who have full time jobs, because when they come home, they have to also look after small children. This situation puts enormous pressure on relationships and affects it in many ways, such as the following:

It kills romance

It kills romance. There is nothing profound about this statement. Cooking day in and day out, washing (including your undies), cleaning, and working in a full time job is not that romantic. Besides the stress and pressure, it also robs people of quality time together. Especially, if a woman's husband is lazy and sits around like a couch potato, doing nothing all the time. In some cases, instead of feeling like she is a man's wife, she may feel like she is a man's mother – and find little difference between looking after you and looking after the children. Once again, it is not a very romantic state of affairs.

It makes her moody.

Sometimes, if all the work in the house, as well as the looking after of the children, is left to a woman, while her husband sits on his bottom, drinks beer, watches TV, goes out with his mates and generally lounges around – it doesn't take much brains to work out that it may just make a woman a little bit moody. She may even start to nag you out of frustration. Unfortunately, many of us men don't always appreciate what is causing our partner to feel that way. Instead, a man grumbles and complains to himself about how his partner always seems to be in a bad mood.

Sometimes he reacts during those times, and this leads to argument and friction.

Woman can lose respect

One significant emotional need a man has is the need for a woman to respect him. Once a relationship deteriorates to the point that respect starts to go out the window, the relationship is probably in grave danger.

A very big way for a man to lose respect from his partner is not to pull his weight around the house, as I have described above – hence the reason why I have included the subject in this chapter.

So what can we do to ease the pressure?

Well, it's simple really. We can help out more with the children, and what needs to be done in the house. Now let me interrupt by saying: while writing about this subject, I have realised that I need to step up myself, and have consequently recently embarked on doing a few projects around the house. The reason for this is because I have been observing a few things happening in my own relationship that I have been just talking about. As the title of this chapter says, it sometimes takes just PLAIN WORK to create a smoother relationship. Fortunately, I am experienced enough to know what is going on, and what I need to do. I have experienced the situation before, and stepped up my work load at that time, and seen how it improves my relationship. Yes, I'm not always consistent, but I believe I am gradually becoming more that way.

No, I'm not saying you should take over the role as main homemaker. Woman, by nature, are busy worker bees, and seem to be always doing something, whether it's dusting, doing their nails, sewing, or changing the house about. Women are natural homemakers, and seem like they operate non-stop 24 hours a day. We are not going to be able to match them, but we can lift our game, do more and take some of the pressure off them. It's called being proactive, and prevents problems occurring in the relationship before they start.

Dear men,

I sincerely hope you have learnt something in this book that will help you in your relationship. It can be a dog's life without this knowledge.

Regards

James

Many thanks to my wonderful wife and two boys, who did the cartoons, and to all the friends who helped with the editing, and gave their support.

About the Great Dr James Dane

James has been happily married for the past 19 years, and has two wonderful children. He attributes recent success in his marriage to constantly threatening his wife by saying: "if she divorces him, she will lose billions of dollars in revenue from future sales of his new book". His wife has never actually read his book, and the only time he caught her looking at a few pages was when she wanted to blackmail him by telling everybody what he wrote in the book, and what he was not doing.

Dr James Dane has a self conferred Ph."Dog" degree, and claims to have gained it through his past animal like behaviour, when he was an innocent young man, and, consequently, being savaged by a few female dogs of "mixed breed".

He read his first book about male/ female relationships when he was about 26 years of age. It was written by a man who incorporated the letters he wrote, to his newly married son, into a book. In the letters, he passed on all the things he had learnt about male/female relationships, and gave many tips. James, at the time, was astounded at what he found because up until then he had treated women like they were men, which to his bewilderment resulted in many strange reactions.

For many years Dr Dane, who is married to a Filipino lady, ran a Filipino pen writing club, and helped many men get to know Filipino ladies and marry.

James is also an accomplished speaker and a gifted comedian. He welcomes being invited to parties, conferences, seminars and church meetings to promote his book, and share some of the information, and he loves free food. He hopes his book will help someone, somewhere, somehow and that he will become rich.

www.ingramcontent.com/pod-product-compliance
Lightning Source LLC
Chambersburg PA
CBHW072044290426
44110CB00014B/1571